Quality assurance in social care

Quality assurance in social care

AN INTRODUCTORY WORKBOOK

Roger Ellis

Dean, Faculty of Social and Health Sciences and Education,
University of Ulster, Northern Ireland

Dorothy Whittington

Senior Lecturer in Health Sciences, University of Ulster, Northern Ireland

ARNOLD

A member of the Hodder Headline Group
LONDON • SYDNEY • AUCKLAND

First published in Great Britain in 1998 by
Arnold, a member of the Hodder Headline Group
338 Euston Road, London NW1 3BH

http://www.arnoldpublishers.com

British Library Cataloguing in Publication Data
A catalogue record for this book is available from the British Library

ISBN 0 340 62509 0

1 2 3 4 5 6 7 8 9 10

Commissioning Editor: Clare Parker
Production Editor: Wendy Rooke
Production Controller: Sarah Kett
Cartoons: Richard Duszczak

Composition in 10/12 Palatino by J&L Composition Ltd, Filey, North Yorkshire
Printed and bound in Great Britain by The Bath Press, Bath

Contents

Acknowledgements

We are grateful to the many colleagues and students whose experience of quality assurance in practice has both informed and challenged our thinking. We are particularly indebted to Katie Campbell and her colleagues of the South and East Belfast Health and Social Services Trust for permission to share their experience of the Fairholme initiative described in Chapter 8, and to Jane Greene and her colleagues of the North Down and Ards Community Health and Social Services Trust for permission to share their experience of the Hospital at Home initiative described in Chapter 9.

About this workbook

Who is this book for?

This workbook is written for people involved in social care, including social workers, care assistants, community health care professionals and voluntary workers. We hope it will be helpful to students approaching initial qualification, and also to lifelong learners already working in social care. Throughout the book, readers will be encouraged to apply ideas to the practice of social care. We have assumed therefore that our readers have some very basic practical knowledge gained from their own practice or from student placement experiences.

What will you achieve by working through this book?

Once you have completed this book we hope that you will:

- understand what quality assurance is;
- know something of the origins of quality assurance;
- appreciate the importance of quality assurance for social care;
- be able to describe a number of quality assurance techniques;
- be able to evaluate the potential of these techniques for your own place of work;
- want to know more about quality assurance;
- be keen to become more involved in quality assurance.

This book is written as a workbook. This means that your own ideas and experience will make a central contribution to each chapter. You will be asked to make notes, work through exercises and carry out practical activities throughout the book. We hope that this will help you to achieve your own personal objectives as well as the ones we have set out above. As a first exercise make notes now (either in the box provided or in a separate notebook) on your own objectives.

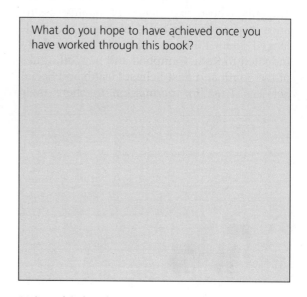

What do you hope to have achieved once you have worked through this book?

Using this book

This book can be used for independent study or for study along with fellow students or colleagues. You can work through it at your own pace, but we suggest that you may find short regular spells of study are more effective than working straight through.

Each chapter and section of this book begins with **objectives** explaining what you should have achieved once you have completed it. You will find it helpful to check your learning against these objectives as you go along. We have also provided brief comments and suggested answers after each **activity**. At four points in the book you will find **self-assessment exercises**. Working through these will help you to revise each part of the book. **Solutions** to these exercises are to be found at the very end of the book. You will also find a **glossary** and a list of **useful books** at the end of the book.

WE HOPE YOU FIND OUR WORKBOOK ENJOYABLE AS WELL AS INSTRUCTIVE.

PART ONE

Understanding quality assurance in social care

Introduction

OBJECTIVES

By the end of Chapter One you will be able to:

- define quality in your own terms;
- define quality assurance in your own terms.

Quality is a word that is commonly used both at work and in other settings. Defining quality can be difficult, however. We begin by asking questions about your own idea of quality.

ACTIVITY 1.1

Write down what you think the word 'quality' means.

You may have met the expression 'quality assurance' at work, in advertisements, or in other places.

ACTIVITY 1.2

Write down what you think 'quality assurance' is.

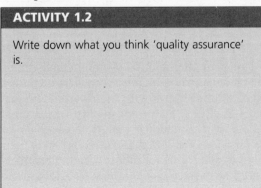

You may have come across quality assurance in your professional life.

ACTIVITY 1.3

Write out your answers to the following.

- What was involved in the quality assurance activity you came across?

- Who began it?

- Who was involved?

- Was it in general a good thing or a bad thing?

- In what way?

Now you have thought about your own ideas concerning 'quality' and 'quality assurance'. In the next chapter we shall consider a number of other views on *quality*.

2 Quality

To help you to understand quality we shall discuss the following questions.

- Why is quality hard to define?
- What are quality standards?
- Who sets quality standards?

2.1 Why is quality hard to define?

Thinking about the quality of everyday products can be a useful introduction to thinking about quality in the more complicated area of social care. Think about buying shoes and try Activity 2.1 now.

Obviously the important characteristics of shoes depend on how they are going to be used. Outdoor walking shoes would have to be waterproof, but it might not matter if high-fashion party shoes were only shower proof. One view

ACTIVITY 2.1

Think about buying shoes. How do you decide which shoes to buy?

You might expect your shoes to be:

- a good fit   ,

- fashionable   ,

- long lasting   ,

- waterproof   ,

- comfortable   ,

- other   ,

          .

Tick the characteristics that would be important to you if you were buying shoes. Add any extra you can think of. Now try putting these characteristics in order of importance, giving the most important the number '1', the next most important '2', and so on.

of quality is that it is the combination of characteristics which make a product *fit for its intended use*.

However, different people might have different views on shoe quality. Teenage purchasers have come to blows with their parents on just that issue! One feature of quality which most people would include is cost. Whether cheap or expensive, most purchasers would like their shoes to give value for money. Quality products would be defined as *fit for their intended use and reasonably priced*.

Now let us pursue this view with another product. This time you are buying a car.

ACTIVITY 2.2

Consider these two situations. Jot down the quality features you would look for in each of them.

- Situation A – you are a family person with a spouse, two children, a dog, and a mortgage which worries you. You are looking for a second car for short runs to the railway station and for occasional local shopping trips.

Quality features:

- Situation B – you are a highly successful business person who makes frequent long trips and needs to impress customers. You have just been promoted and are replacing your current car.

Quality features:

In situation A, the car needs to be reasonably priced, cheap to run and maintain, and as large, comfortable and reliable as possible. Style and appearance are less important. In situation B, the business person's car needs to be luxurious, powerful, quiet, stylish and reliable. It may well

be expensive, but that is less important as its high price will impress business customers.

The car in situation B is what is commonly called a 'quality car'. This view of quality implies a *high-quality rating on all or nearly all features* and, usually, high cost. It ignores the intended use of the car. A basic car cannot be regarded as a quality product even if it is superbly designed and manufactured, never breaks down and is very cheap to run, service and maintain. However, if quality means being fit for the intended use and reasonably priced, then in situation A the basic car could be rated higher in quality than a Rolls-Royce.

These simple examples have shown that quality can be defined in different ways, and that the quality of any product depends on its purpose and on the setting in which it will be used.

ACTIVITY 2.3

Find a dictionary and look at the definitions it gives for the word 'quality'. Jot down ways in which the dictionary definitions differ from those you have considered so far.

Your dictionary probably suggested that although the word 'quality' often suggests something 'good' or 'excellent', its basic meaning is more neutral. Quality can be poor or mediocre as well as good, or low or unacceptable as well as high or desirable. In the strictest sense the 'quality' of something is the collection of characteristics which distinguish it from other things.

ACTIVITY 2.4

Make a list of characteristics which describe the 'quality' of snow.

Almost everyone asked to describe the quality of snow uses the words 'white' and 'cold'. People who have experience of skiing or who live in countries where heavy snowfalls are common make longer and more technical lists. Even in this neutral sense, definitions of quality are not simple.

As you may have realized, so far in this book we have not been using the word 'quality' in this basic, neutral way. We have been thinking of quality as a *positive* characteristic. It is this positive idea of quality that can be defined as 'fit for the intended purpose'.

Now consider some different examples.

ACTIVITY 2.5

In your own work setting there are some professionals you admire for the quality of their work. Think of a member of your own profession, a colleague perhaps, who seems to you to be a high-quality professional.

Write down the characteristics which led you to choose this person.

Once again, you have produced your idea of positive quality in a given situation. Your view is influenced by your professional background, area of work, status, and work environment.

You may have used words like:

Committed, caring, co-operative;
Accountable, approachable, autonomous;
Reliable, resourceful, reflective;
Expert, efficient, ethical.

These characteristics describe a competent practitioner, but they do not describe the service that is provided. The following are some characteristics that you might include if you were asked to describe a quality service in your own area of expertise:

Comprehensive, cost-effective, client-centred;
Accessible, acceptable, affordable;
Relevant, reliable, responsive;
Efficient, equitable, effective.

ACTIVITY 2.6

Choose the quality characteristics in the list we have given which you think are important aspects of the service delivered in your own place of work. Add any others you can think of.

Now try to place them in order of importance.

You may find it helpful to discuss your list with friends or colleagues who work in similar settings.

You probably found that exercise more difficult than the earlier exercises on shoes and cars. If you discussed your list with colleagues you may have disagreed with them. The definition and description of quality in social care depend on who is defining and describing it, what they think social care is for, and their understanding of the setting in which it is to be provided.

In this section you have considered some of the problems encountered in defining quality. You have begun to consider the definition of quality in social care.

2.2 What are quality standards?

OBJECTIVES

After working through this section you will be able to:

- describe the relationship between standards and quality;

- outline different frameworks for standard setting.

ACTIVITY 2.7

Write down what you mean by the term 'standard'.

In Section 2.1 you listed characteristics that, in your opinion, described quality shoes. Your imagined aim was to buy shoes that satisfied your requirements against each of those characteristics. Your requirements were related to the way in which the shoes would be used. For example, walking shoes have to stay dry in a downpour, but fashion shoes might not have to. In other words, the *standard* of waterproofing that you find acceptable depends on the type of shoe and its intended purpose. You have in mind different degrees of resistance to rain against which you would judge the quality of different types of shoes. These are your *standards*.

In social care, too, quality is determined in relation to standards. Here is a definition of a standard which one profession found helpful.

'A standard is an acceptable or approved example or statement of something against which measurement and/or judgement takes place; a level of quality relevant to the activity'.

This definition was developed by the College of Occupational Therapists, but it could easily apply to standards for a wide range of social care activities.

The definition makes it clear that a standard must:

- be approved or accepted by relevant groups;
- specify what has to be achieved;
- specify the level of achievement required;
- allow for measurement or judgement that the specified level has been achieved.

The following is an example of a standard:

'90 per cent of older people referred for managed care assessment will have had their needs assessed and will have a preliminary care plan in place within 4 weeks of referral.'

Achieved performance is compared with the standard set. If, in our example, records show that 30 per cent of clients wait longer than 4 weeks for their assessment, or if assessments are not followed up by care planning, then the standard is not being met. Managers can deal with this situation in at least two ways. Changes could be made in the service so that the standard is met more often. In this case it might be necessary to review communication between staff carrying out assessments, or to simplify recording systems. On the other hand it might be decided that the target is unachievable within existing resources. In that case the standard would have to be changed.

Standards could be set for many different aspects of quality. A number of frameworks have been developed which help to organize standard setting. They identify aspects of care within which quality – and standard setting – can be categorized.

In an early attempt to measure health care quality, Donabedian (1966) proposed three categories into which service could be divided – *structure*, *process* and *outcome*. They are widely used in quality assurance in health and social care, and also in other professional areas such as law and accountancy.

- **Structure** – the resources devoted to care.
- **Process** – the activities of care.
- **Outcome** – the results of care.

Structure standards could be set for personnel, equipment, buildings, record systems, finance, supplies, facilities, etc. Process standards might be for activities that involve clients directly or for activities such as record keeping, which are about clients but do not involve them face to face. Outcome standards might be for relatively short-term results (e.g. managed care assessments completed within 4 weeks) or for much more long-term results (e.g. a specified group of older people supported in living at home for a period of years).

All three categories need to be considered to obtain an overall view of quality. For example, it does not automatically follow that a quality service will be delivered just because there is a purpose-built environment.

Another framework developed from industrial and other sources (Maxwell, 1984; Juran, 1988) is as follows.

- **Timeliness** – access, waiting and action time.

- **Information** – clarification, explanation and client involvement.
- **Technical competence** – knowledge, skills and expertise.
- **Interpersonal competence** – personal interaction between practitioner and client.
- **Environment** – buildings, amenities, maintenance and cleanliness.

Norfolk Social Services Department (James, 1992) found it helpful to categorize their quality objectives as follows.

- **Client focus**.
- **Prompt response to clients**.
- **Appropriate response to clients**.
- **Client involvement in decision-making**.
- **Effective and imaginative use of resources**.
- **Satisfaction of client need**.

ACTIVITY 2.8

You are visiting your dentist. Against each category of care write down what is important to you as a client, and try to specify a standard for the care you would like to receive.

CATEGORY   STANDARD

Timeliness

Information

Technical competence

Interpersonal competence

Environment

In trying to specify acceptable levels of service you probably discovered that some categories were easier than others. Waiting time is easy to measure, so it is easy to set an acceptable limit on it. What limits did you specify? Measurements of time are said to be *objective*. Distance travelled by clients, number of clients seen per day, number of staff employed, and

incidence of pressure sores in nursing home patients are further examples of objective measures. Objective measures can be easily agreed upon and can be compared with each other.

But how did you set a standard for the dentist's interpersonal competence? Or for the information given to you? These things are less easy to measure and judgements made about their quality are more likely to be *subjective* or to depend on personal perception.

ACTIVITY 2.9

Look back at the lists of characteristics you made in Section 2.1 describing quality shoes and then quality social care.

How many of these characteristics could be measured objectively?

Most (but not all) aspects of shoe quality could be objectively measured. Social care quality presents more difficulty.

In health care quality assurance, some professionals have found it useful to set separate standards for *technical*, *interpersonal* and *moral* aspects of care.

- **Technical** – involving physical interventions.
- **Interpersonal** – involving interaction and relationships between people.
- **Moral** – involving ethical decisions.

ACTIVITY 2.10

Go back to your list of characteristics of social care quality and try to categorize them as technical, interpersonal or moral. (You will probably find that some fall into more than one category.)

For which will it be easiest to set objectively measurable standards?

• Now try to set a standard in each of these categories for an aspect of your own professional work.

CATEGORY   STANDARD

Timeliness

Information

Technical competence

Interpersonal competence

Environment

Clients, professionals, managers, local authorities, voluntary and private agencies all have different views on quality. These different perspectives depend on knowledge, experience and overall aims. They also depend on the situation. For example, a client who needs advice on benefits and financial support may place more value on the social worker's technical knowledge than on their interpersonal skill. On the other hand, a client coming to terms with a spouse's Alzheimer's disease may value empathy and understanding as highly as technical knowledge.

In isolation, the various interested parties would judge quality on the basis of different standards. It is therefore important to consider who sets the standards.

In this section you have explored the relationship between standards and quality. You have found out about a number of frameworks for setting standards. You have also discovered that views of quality can vary.

Technical standards are easiest to measure objectively. Social care is even more dependent on interpersonal relationships and ethical judgements than health care. Both social and health care professionals have worked with social scientists to try to produce more objective measures of these features of quality.

ACTIVITY 2.11

• Go back to the standards you set for your visit to the dentist. This time imagine you are the dentist. The categories of care are still important to you, but perhaps you have different expectations now that you are looking at the situation from the professional's viewpoint.

Figure 2.1 A quality chain

2.3 Who sets quality standards in social care?

OBJECTIVES

After working through this section you will be able to:

- describe a quality 'chain' in your own workplace;

- identify individuals and groups who are 'stakeholders' in quality social care;

- discuss who should take responsibility for quality.

In Section 2.1 we considered the quality of manufactured products such as shoes and cars. We examined their quality from the point of view of various customers. However, there are other people who would have an interest. They include the retailer, wholesaler, distributor, manufacturer and manufacturer's suppliers. Each person in the chain has an interest in providing a quality product to you the consumer or client. If you are not satisfied with the quality of your purchase you will complain, return the product or buy elsewhere in future. Your dissatisfaction will have an impact on the business success of each person in the quality chain. Notice that some people in the chain act both as a customer and as a supplier. The retailer is your supplier but also the wholesaler's customer.

In large organizations each section or department has internal customers and internal suppliers. Quality standards are often set for the products or services delivered inside the one organization. In the National Health Service, and increasingly in the organization of social services, some customer – supplier relationships have been formalized. The customer and supplier are called the purchaser and the provider respectively, formal contracts are agreed between them and money changes hands. In social care the purchaser is usually the local authority and providers can be statutory, voluntary or private agencies. Quality is an important aspect of all of these contractual arrangements, and formal quality standards are often set. Taken together these standards are sometimes referred to as a patients' or clients' *charter*.

The quality chain in social care is often complex. The client is the customer. All members of the care team work together to provide a quality service for clients, but it is important to remember that each team member may be a customer of other members. For example, when residential care workers encourage residents to eat unaided they use the food produced by the kitchen staff and are therefore their customers. Quality in the kitchen will affect the quality of care given to the clients. If the food is cold or unpalatable, the clients' capacity for self-care may be less likely to improve.

ACTIVITY 2.12

Choose one of your professional practice areas and list your customers and your suppliers.

You may be able to identify points in your own chain of customers and suppliers where problems or conflicts occur. Conflicts may occur through inadequate resources, unsuitable accommodation, insufficient support staff or poor communication. Any of these can make appropriate quality standards difficult to maintain. Some questions naturally follow such a statement. You may ask, for example, what the word 'appropriate' means. This question will be addressed in the next section. Here it is noted that it is easy to blame problems on the lack of resources. Without doubt some quality problems can be attributed to this, but not all of them. This, too, will be discussed later.

Now we shall return to the question of who sets the quality standards.

In social care, quality involves relationships between numerous groups of professional and lay people.

ACTIVITY 2.13

Consider one of your current clients. Make a list of all the people who could influence the quality of care that he or she receives.

A wide range of individuals directly and indirectly associated with your client could influence the quality of care. You have probably included in your list the professionals and volunteers who provide care on an individual basis, and those whose work is essential in the provision of an overall quality service (for example, clerical and administrative staff). If we add relatives involved in informal care, community agencies and local pressure groups, we can see the size of the network that affects the quality of care for a single client.

Quality of care is important to clients, professionals and managers, and to society as a whole. Each group may be interested in quality for different reasons and will have different priorities. Their interests may be purely client-centred, or influenced by external pressures such as government policy, scarcity of resources or changing technology. As a result they will have different perspectives on quality. The above diagram is a simplified representation of the relationship between clients, professionals, managers and policy-makers. All of them are major stakeholders in quality.

At an individual level, everyone affects the quality of social care – receptionists, telephonists, drivers, building maintenance staff, managers, clerical staff, caterers, volunteers and professional staff. Professional staff, too, may include different groups – social workers, care assistants, community nurses, occupational therapists, physiotherapists, chiropodists and general practitioners may all be members of the care team. **Quality is everyone's business**.

There is a potential problem here. Since quality is everyone's business, it can become no one's business. Someone needs to take responsibility for quality. Many Social Services Departments and voluntary agencies designate individuals who have overall responsibility.

This helps to ensure that quality matters are regularly considered and are taken seriously.

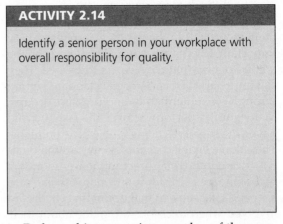

Perhaps this person is a member of the management board or a senior member of your professional group. It is likely that this person will be in the process of constructing policy documents and local initiatives in relation to quality assurance. One problem is that once someone becomes known as 'the quality person,' other people may forget that quality is everyone's business.

Everyone who accepts that they contribute to quality sets personal standards. These personal standards are informal and are seldom written down or seen by anyone else. Individuals judge their performance against their own ideal. Many judgements are subjective.

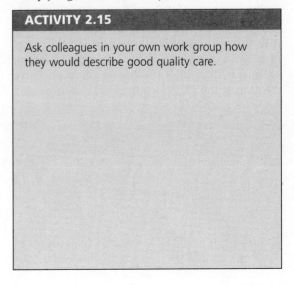

You will probably find some common features across the replies. Many of the features may be difficult to measure objectively.

Clients are on the receiving end of care, and their view of the service they receive is very important. Clients set informal standards on the quality of care that they expect to receive. They can indirectly influence formal standard setting through consumer bodies and pressure groups. Many studies performed over the last 10 years have investigated clients' subjective opinions. These have enabled clients' views on the quality of care to have a direct influence upon formal standards. In addition, many social care agencies take steps to make sure that clients are involved when decisions are made about their care.

Professionals are also involved in setting standards for the care of individual clients or specified groups of clients. All professional bodies are responsible for setting basic or *threshold* standards of competence. The quality of professional activity must not fall below these standards. They are the basis of the professional's licence to practise.

Standards for client care are sometimes set by interprofessional teams. In this way potential conflicts between professional perspectives can be discussed and resolved.

Many health-related professional bodies have produced comprehensive standards documents. Interprofessional standards setting groups have to ensure that their standards comply with these specifications. The Royal College of Nursing (RCN) has taken a different approach. Instead of producing comprehensive standards, the RCN produced a system within which local groups of nurses can set their own standards. It is called the Dynamic Standard Setting System (DySSSy) (Royal College of Nursing, 1990).

In this section you have explored what is meant by internal customers and suppliers. You have also discovered that a range of people have an interest in the determination of social care quality.

Now that you have completed Chapter 2, go back to the ideas of quality you had when you finished Chapter 1. You should find that your ideas have changed.

ACTIVITY 2.16

- Write a definition of quality.

- What are its strengths?

- What are its weaknesses?

Self-Assessment Exercises

Now that you have completed Chapters 1 and 2 you may find it helpful to check your progress by trying these self-assessment exercises. You will find our suggested answers at the of the book.

Exercise 1

Complete the following sentences by choosing a word or phrase from those listed.

1. Product quality is often defined as _____.
   complex
   cheap
   fit for purpose
   neutral quality

2. Definition of quality in social care depends in part on _____.
   who is defining it
   how equitable it is
   competent practitioners
   standards

3. The quality of care is often determined by comparing achieved quality with _____.
   neutral quality
   standards
   specificity
   price

4. In Donabedian's categorization of care, 'structure' refers to _____.
   the resources devoted to care
   the number of carers
   the way in which different carers communicate with each other
   organization

5. Objective standards are _____ than subjective standards.
   more acceptable
   less interpersonal
   easier to measure
   less complex

6. Each person in a quality chain _____.
   has set standards
   has an interest in the quality of the product or service
   has a formal contract
   has one customer

Exercise 2

Which of the following statements are true? Write true or false in the space provided.

1. Price has nothing to do with quality.

   _____

2. Quality means excellence.

   _____

3. Standards state what has to be achieved.

   _____

4. Care process is face-to-face care.

   _____

5. Subjective standards should never be used.

   _____

6. Professional bodies set threshold standards of competence.

   _____

Exercise 3

1. Give two reasons why standards might be difficult to set in social care.

2. Give two reasons why it might be a bad thing to have one named person responsible for quality in your own workplace.

3. Give two reasons why clients should be involved in quality assurance for social care.

Exercise 4

Write definitions of the following:

1. quality;
2. standards;
3. outcome quality.

Now that you have completed these exercises, check your answers with the solutions at the end of the book.

3 Quality assurance

OBJECTIVES

By the end of Chapter Three you will be able to:

- provide a definition of quality assurance;
- discuss the importance of quality assurance in social care;
- outline the historical development of quality assurance;
- discuss aspects of the relationship between quality and cost;
- list some sources of information about quality assurance.

To help you to achieve these objectives we shall consider the following questions.

- What is quality assurance?
- Why is quality assurance needed in social care?
- How did quality assurance develop?
- What does quality cost?
- How can you find out more about quality assurance?

3.1 What is quality assurance?

OBJECTIVES

After working through this section you will be able to-

- suggest a definition of quality assurance.

You have seen that quality is a complex concept which can be difficult to define. It should come as no surprise therefore that there is no universally agreed definition of quality assurance.

Your dictionary may use words such as 'promise', 'guarantee' and 'confidence'. How do these relate to the quality of care?

ACTIVITY 3.1

Using your dictionary, make a note of the definition of the following words.

- Assure

- Assurance

Quality assurance provides evidence that gives clients or customers confidence that the quality of a product or service will consistently satisfy stated requirements. The product or service will be up to standard. In social care, quality assurance provides evidence of the standard of service that clients can expect. It provides a *guarantee*.

At a basic level this involves:

- setting standards;
- appraising actual achievements.

Setting standards involves writing statements that describe achievable and desirable levels of quality. They set out the professionals' expectations of the service and indicate to clients what it is that the professionals intend to provide. Appraising actual achievement involves comparing practice with the stated standards using both measurement and judgement. If standards are consistently met, this may be all that is required to provide clients with a guarantee. From time to time, however, standards will not be met. Clients can only be fully assured of quality if the following stages are also included:

- planning for improvement;
- taking action when required.

Any gap between expectation and achievement requires action to be taken. This involves planning for improvement. If quality of care is below the stated acceptable levels, then action must be taken to raise quality until standards are met.

Quality assurance is a continuous process. Comparison is made periodically which enables the effects of changes to be monitored. If provision is level with or above expectation, then the standard may be changed to specify an even higher level of service quality.

These basic stages are commonly referred to as the *quality cycle*. They are shown in Figure 3.1

Quality assurance leads to a never-ending improvement in the quality of care. The repetition of the cycle can be viewed as a spiral rising to the ultimate quality service. This is shown in Figure 3.2.

In order to be successful, quality assurance must be organized and managed through a structured system. The system should ensure that quality assurance is not just talked about, that action for improvement as well as quality appraisal takes place, and that activities are documented and reported.

ACTIVITY 3.2

Think about what is needed to support quality assurance initiatives. Put a tick against each of the following features if you think it is important.

- Accurate and up-to-date documentation
- Effective communication
- Willingness to change
- Training for quality assurance activities
- Commitment from top management
- Commitment from all personnel
- Clear responsibilities for quality activities

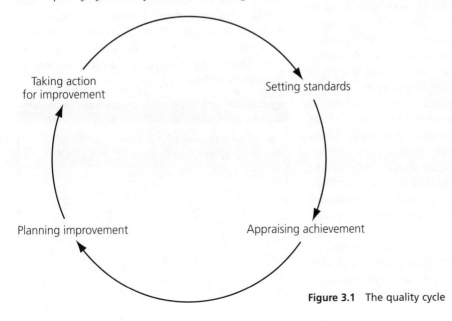

Figure 3.1 The quality cycle

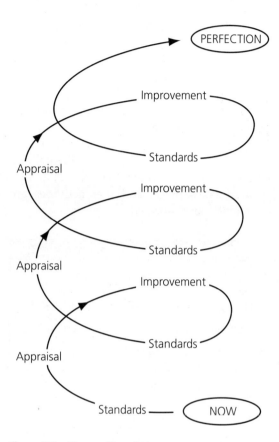

Figure 3.2   The quality spiral

There ought to be ticks against every feature.

Clear, detailed and accurate records need to be maintained on procedures to be followed, actions to be taken and actions actually taken.

Effective communication at all levels means that people are well informed, and the right people have the right information at the right time and in the right place. Good communication is often vital when change is taking place. Many people find change threatening. Good communication can help.

Training programmes on quality help to foster commitment to quality assurance They introduce people to quality techniques that are needed to enable them to take part in quality assurance initiatives.

Top management needs to be committed so that resources are allocated to quality assurance initiatives and actions are followed through. However, quality is influenced by everyone, so

it is important that all staff are committed to improvement and are willing to accept and implement change. People need to know what they are expected to do, so responsibilities for quality activities must be clearly assigned.

But why do social care professionals need to be involved in quality assurance? Indeed, why is quality assurance becoming more common in social care?

3.2 Why is quality assurance needed in social care?

OBJECTIVES

After working through this section you will be able to :

● identify quality assurance systems and procedures in your own workplace;

● identify and discuss a number of reasons for the increasing importance of quality assurance in social care.

In previous sections we discussed definitions of quality and quality assurance, and we spent some time discussing standards. As you worked through these sections you probably thought about how these ideas related to your own work. Perhaps you thought of aspects of your work where there is a formal system of quality assurance.

ACTIVITY 3.3

● Make a note of all the areas of your own work where there is some form of quality assurance.

- Make a note of other areas of social care where you know there is some form of quality assurance.

You probably thought of the work of the Social Services Inspection Units, and possibly of complaints procedures. There are many other forms of quality assurance in social care, but their use has only recently been becoming widespread.

ACTIVITY 3.4

- List four reasons why quality assurance in social care is increasing in importance.

Quality assurance is steadily increasing in importance in social care for a large number of reasons. They can be grouped into three main

categories each of which will now be considered in turn.

PROFESSIONAL FACTORS

Conduct and Competence

All professions have Codes of Conduct or statements about professional behaviour which outline professional rules. Boundaries are set for acceptable practice. If you, as a practitioner, operate outside your code of conduct, you may be disciplined and your licence to practise may be withdrawn. In social care the Central Council for the Education and Training of Social Workers (CCETSW) has recently been very active in establishing guidelines and standards for non-discriminatory practice. Professional bodies are also responsible for standards of training and qualification for practice. CCETSW works with universities and colleges to make sure that students qualifying with their awards have reached appropriate standards in specified areas of competence. New structures of awards have recently led to review of these professional competences.

Accountability and Identity

In recent years there has been much public debate about the effectiveness of social care. Professionals themselves have often asked questions about the way in which services are organized and resourced. Professional organizations have found it helpful to highlight their commitment to a consistent and accountable service – a major aim of a quality assurance system.

Recent changes in the way in which community care is organized have led to increased interprofessional activity. Good interprofessional relationships have often been helped by discussion of each profession's aims and values, and

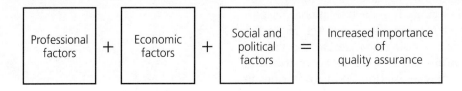

by joint standard setting for service delivery and for interprofessional communication.

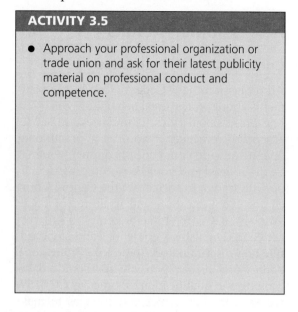

ACTIVITY 3.5

- Approach your professional organization or trade union and ask for their latest publicity material on professional conduct and competence.

ECONOMIC FACTORS

Increasing Demand for Care

Nationally and internationally people are living longer and are surviving with serious illness and disability. An increasing number of dependent people require both health and social care which must be paid for by people who are economically active. This has become a sensitive political issue. There is thus a growing need for services which give value for money while maintaining quality standards.

Distribution of Resources for Care

Different countries control and distribute resources for care in different ways. Social care in the USA is largely provided through private insurance systems. In the UK there has been a long tradition of provision through central and local government agencies and through the voluntary sector. The 1990 National Health Service and Community Care Act of Parliament made sweeping changes to the way in which care resources were to be distributed. Under this new legislation Local Authorities in England and Wales became responsible for the co-ordination of community care through a 'mixed economy' of statutory, voluntary and private provision. In health care the Regional Health Authorities (and also fund-holding general practitioners) became 'purchasers' of care using the resources allocated to them to commission care from hospitals and other agencies. Many Local Authorities have also adopted this model and establish formal contracts with agencies providing social care. These contracts generally have clauses setting out required standards of service quality.

The 1997 white paper entitled 'The New NHS' (Department of Health, 1997) recommends even stronger links between Local Authority social service departments and the health service. It also makes it clear that the distribution of resources for care will be closely related to the development of explicit quality standards and quality assurance procedures.

ACTIVITY 3.6

- Find out whether the service you are involved with is organized through a system of contracting.

- If it is, ask your line manager or other responsible person about service quality agreements.

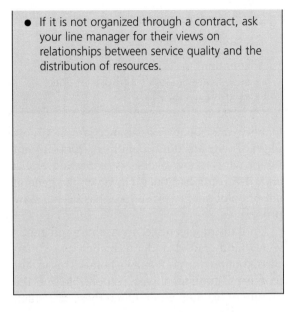

- If it is not organized through a contract, ask your line manager for their views on relationships between service quality and the distribution of resources.

ACTIVITY 3.7

- List three ways in which your own clients are (or could be) involved in improving their own care.

SOCIAL AND POLITICAL FACTORS

Public Awareness

The public generally are increasingly well informed about their rights as consumers. This applies to social care as much as to anything else. Clients have access to complaints procedures, to the Ombudsman or even to legal proceedings when an unacceptable level of service is received. Where particularly poor service comes to light, or where there has been professional misconduct, the result is often national publicity through the media. The establishment of additional or improved quality assurance procedures is a common response to 'scandals' of this kind.

Client Involvement

Client feedback on the quality of service is increasingly seen as a simple but effective source of ideas for its improvement. In some areas of social care, legislation requires local authorities to involve clients (and their informal carers) in designing the package of care they are to receive. Both of these forms of client involvement can lead to the setting of quality standards.

Legislation

Social care is provided by statutory, voluntary and private agencies. Whoever provides it, they do so in a framework of legislation. From Queen Elizabeth the First's 'Poor Law' through to the 1990 NHS and Community Care Act, the organization and funding of social care have been regulated by laws. Many of these laws also set broad standards for the way in which services were to be delivered.

The 1990 reforms of health and social care included the establishment of quality systems. In health care, all professions were required to set up 'audit systems' which would provide for regular review of service standards. The social care reforms did not require that kind of audit. Instead, local authority Social Services departments were required to set up 'Inspection Units'. These Units register and inspect residential care homes for children and adults, day services for children under 8 years of age, and the welfare of children in boarding schools. The Units inspect services, whoever provides them. They are required to do so as objectively and independently as possible, and are often called 'arm's-length' units.

Although various government publications *encourage* other quality assurance systems in social care, they are not *required* by law. Recent government statements on quality in social care suggest that local authorities may soon be required to review their quality assurance systems in all areas of social and community care.

In this section, we have outlined many reasons for the increasing importance of quality assurance in social care. They include professional, economic and social/political factors. One study of quality assurance in Social Services Departments (James, 1992) found that managers and professionals thought that quality assurance would help them to:

- demonstrate value for money;
- demonstrate achievement of policy objectives;
- improve the experience of the service user;
- manage change within their Department.

ACTIVITY 3.8

- Return to your earlier list of reasons for the increasing importance of quality assurance in social care. See how many more reasons you can now add.

- Go through your longer list and put a tick by each reason that would apply in your own workplace.

Now that you know what quality assurance is and why it is increasingly important in social care, you are ready to find out how it developed.

3.3 How did quality assurance develop?

OBJECTIVES

After working through this section you will be able to:

- trace the development of quality assurance in industry;

- trace the development of quality assurance in health care;

- comment on how quality assurance in social care relates to industrial and health care models.

Quality and quality assurance are not new ideas. There are tomb paintings from ancient Egypt which show overseers inspecting bricks and discarding bad ones. However, the general adoption of quality procedures has been a slow process.

Until the nineteenth century almost all goods were hand-crafted and production was often carried out in the craftsman's home. This meant that each craftsman was responsible for the quality of his own work. Often these craftsmen knew their customers personally and were able to discuss quality with them. Where goods were being distributed more widely there were other systems for maintaining standards. In the Middle Ages the merchant guilds trained apprentices, disciplined guildsmen who broke codes of practice, and offered guarantees of quality. For example, cloth bearing the Colchester guild mark was renowned for its high quality throughout England and other parts of Europe.

After the Industrial Revolution, goods were more likely to be produced in factories. Workers were unlikely to know their customers personally and often were only responsible for a small part of the production process. Other methods of ensuring quality were required. Systems of *inspection* were introduced. The inspectors were responsible for examining goods coming to the end of the production line. They picked out shoddy goods and either sent them to be brought up to standard or threw them away. In this period, too, it became important to manufacture goods and parts of goods to very precise specifications. Railway lines manufactured in different places and at different times had to fit together properly. Professional organizations of engineers began to take responsibility for the uniformity and consistent quality of such materials. This led to the idea of national stan-

An early approach to guaranteeing food quality

dards and the creation of the British Standards Institution.

During the 1930s and 1940s some companies developed and used statistical techniques to monitor the quality of goods coming off the production line. This was called *quality control*. After the Second World War, quality control experts from the USA were sent to Japan to help to restore Japanese industry. The Japanese were enthusiastic learners and worked with their American colleagues to develop new techniques and approaches including *quality assurance*, *quality circles* and *total quality management*. Quality assurance systems were designed so that no poor-quality goods would be produced. Each worker was once more responsible for the quality of his own work, and there was to be no need for inspectors at the end of the production line.

These approaches to quality played a significant role in establishing the Japanese economy as one of the most successful in the world. In the rapidly developing electronics industry the Japanese overtook and out-performed all competitors as a direct result of their high-quality standards. In the West, the quality assurance approach was first adopted in connection with NATO defence contracts. Instead of standards being set for products themselves, they were set for quality assurance *systems* covering the processes of design, manufacture, inspection and testing. These NATO standards formed the basis of the first version of British Standard (BS) 5750. A firm which has been awarded BS5750 has provided evidence that it has specified a quality system and is working to it. Later versions of this British standard were the basis for the international quality standard ISO 9000.

ACTIVITY 3.9

The quality techniques you have just learned about were developed for maintaining and improving the quality of manufactured goods. List aspects of social care to which they could be applied directly.

You may have mentioned activities like laundry or meals-on-wheels services, or even record-keeping. In all of these cases, standards could be set for a physical object which could be examined and assessed by independent observers at any time. Many social care activities, however, are primarily interpersonal. These cannot be produced for examination in the same way. However, this does not mean that quality assurance will not work in these areas. Techniques have been developed in service industries (like catering, tourism or entertainment) where face-to-face communication with customers is very important. Health care quality assurance has also adopted these techniques – particularly in primary and community health care where there are close links with social care.

As early as the sixteenth century the founding charter of the Royal College of Physicians stated that its members would 'uphold standards for the public benefit'. More recently, the General Medical Council and the various professional bodies for nursing and other health-related professions have taken responsibility for regulation of education and training, admission and registration, and discipline. Until very recently, however, few provided anything beyond the broadest guidelines for the delivery of sound quality care by qualified members of the profession.

In the USA there has been systematic quality assurance in health care since the early years of this century. Hospitals' patient records are examined by an independent body, and if standards of care are acceptable they are awarded 'accreditation'. Records are also examined before hospitals are allowed to take patients whose bills are met through state-supported or charitable health insurance systems. This tradition of quality assurance has led to the development of techniques for the review of selected cases (Ellis and Whittington, 1993). Many could easily be adapted for use in social care.

In the UK many health-related professional bodies anticipated the 1990 government requirement for audit by setting up their own quality initiatives. The Royal College of Nursing set up its 'Standards of Care' project as early as 1965, and The Royal College of General Practitioners launched its initiative in 1985. Guidelines and standards have been produced by the professional bodies for physiotherapy, occupational therapy, dietetics, pharmacy, speech and language therapy, and podiatry. In medicine itself, most of the specialist Colleges have produced audit guidelines and protocols for treatment of specified conditions. In addition to these professional activities, most health care trusts and regional authorities have encouraged the development of quality systems. Several have obtained quality 'kitemarks' such as BS5750 or accreditation through the organizational audit scheme sponsored by the King's Fund.

It is clear that both government and the professions have recognized the importance of quality assurance in health care. The 1997 white paper entitled 'The New NHS' (Department of Health, 1997) explicitly proposes 'a new drive for quality' and recommends national standards and guidelines, local measures for quality improvement and a new national organization to address shortcomings. Quality assurance is now well established in all areas of the National Health Service and in private practice. It is likely that the next few years will see similar developments in social care.

ACTIVITY 3.10

- Ask a colleague or friend who is a health professional what they know of quality assurance in their own profession.

- Ask the same colleague or friend how they have been involved in quality assurance in their own workplace.

- Make notes on how health care quality assurance techniques might be adapted for use in your own profession and workplace.

3.4 How are quality and cost related?

By the end of this section you will be able to:

- identify costs associated with poor quality;

- identify costs associated with quality systems;

- discuss the meaning of cost-effectiveness.

In manufacturing industry, costs associated with poor quality include *product failure* costs and *process failure* costs.

Product failure costs include the cost of reprocessing or discarding poor-quality goods detected through inspection or quality control. They also include the costs of reduced sales resulting from consumers buying poor-quality products and warning other people not to deal with the company.

Process failure costs are associated with inefficient use of material or human resources. This can happen through waste or unnecessary bureaucracy. It can also be the result of employing staff with inappropriate or limited knowledge and skills. Poor communication between individual staff or groups of staff is a common source of poor process quality. High-quality goods can be produced by companies with poor-quality processes – but they cost more than they should.

In service industries and health care, costs associated with poor outcome quality are the equivalent of poor product quality. They can include costs associated with:

- customer/patient complaint and compensation;
- customers/patients going to law;
- customers/patients requiring additional service or treatment;

- customers/patients going elsewhere for future service;
- poor public reputation created by dissatisfied customers/patients.

Process failure costs in service industries and health care are very similar to those in manufacturing industries. Again it is possible to deliver a high-quality service – but at extra cost.

ACTIVITY 3.11

Make a list of costs of the following.

- Poor outcome quality in social care;

- Poor process quality in social care.

In both health and social care, poor quality care can have long-term costs. Poor child care may lead to adult problems which require further care and support. Stress caused to a poorly supported informal carer may lead to illness many years later.

ACTIVITY 3.12

Poor quality is often blamed on lack of resources. Think of an example of poor-quality service you have encountered in your own working life. Now answer the following questions.

- How would additional resources have improved quality?

- How could quality have been improved *without* extra resources?

You have discovered that poor quality costs money. Setting up systems to avoid the costs of poor quality also costs money. Effective quality assurance systems cost less than the costs of the poor quality they prevent.

ACTIVITY 3.13

Think of a client you have recently been involved with. Try to make a complete list of the costs associated with the care provided.

NB Have you included costs of any informal care provided by relatives, friends or neighbours?

Poor quality always costs money. Good quality need not do so.

Overall costs in social care are particularly difficult to track. Care is often delivered by a range of different professionals and agencies. These may be funded through state or charitable support, or may depend on direct client payment. Each of these may charge differently for the same service. Finally, different Local Authorities may manage care in different ways with different balances of private, voluntary and statutory involvement.

Costs of quality assurance systems include costs of:

- development of standards;
- development and operation of systems for reviewing performance;
- development and operation of systems for improving performance;
- education and training of staff for quality assurance.

We have already noticed that tracking the costs of social care can be complex. In earlier sections we identified some of the problems in specifying quality in social care. Policy-makers and professionals are faced with the difficult task of deciding how best to provide high quality social care at reasonable cost – *a cost-effective service*.

ACTIVITY 3.14

You are a social services manager considering establishing a new dementia day care service. Which of the following options should you decide to pursue?

- A low-cost/low-quality service
- A high-cost/low-quality service
- A low-cost/high-quality service
- A high-cost/high-quality service

Of course you chose the third option – high quality at low cost is every manager's dream. In real life, however, choices are rarely so simple. It may not be possible to determine predicted cost and quality levels with enough confidence. And how should you choose if the only options are low cost and low quality on the one hand and high cost and high quality on the other? Economists who have studied social care costs have tried to develop ways of disentangling different aspects of both costs and quality (Knapp, 1984; Wistow et al, 1996). Managers, professionals and policy-makers who use these methods can at least make more informed judgements.

3.5 Where can information about quality assurance be found?

OBJECTIVES

By the end of this section you will be able to:

- identify some local and national sources of information;
- identify key individuals who may be able to help.

You may already know some ways of obtaining information about quality assurance.

ACTIVITY 3.15

Start an alphabetical directory (you could use an address book) of sources of information. We hope this will be useful long after you have completed this workbook.

Sources that you may have considered include:

Literature

Information about quality assurance can be found in all of the following:

- UK, European and world-wide books, journals and articles;
- professional newsletters and magazines;
- national reports publishing results of specific studies;
- local social services newsletters and reports;
- local health service newsletters and reports;
- government reports available from HMSO bookshops;
- King's Fund Centre bibliographic service documents;
- National Institute for Social Work reports
- reports from the Social Work Research Centre, University of Stirling;
- reports from the Personal Social Services Research Unit (University of Kent/London School of Economics);
- reports from charities and other voluntary sector agencies.

Organizations

All of the following organizations can supply information about quality assurance in industry, health care or social care.

- the British Standards Institution – an accreditation body for the national (and international) standard on quality assurance;
- the Department of Trade and Industry – provides some publications free on request;
- the Institute of Quality Assurance – concerned with the promotion of quality in manufacturing, production and service industries;

- the Central Council for the Education and Training of Social Workers;
- the British Association of Social Workers;
- the National Institute for Social Work;
- the King's Fund Centre – provides a Quality Assurance Information Service and an Information Exchange scheme;
- Universities or colleges.

Training opportunities

Courses, study days and conferences are organized and provided by the following:

- professional bodies – organised as monoprofessional or interprofessional events at local and national levels;
- Social Services Departments;
- Health Authorities and Trusts;
- universities and colleges (often as part of accredited post-qualifying education) – short courses, undergraduate courses, postgraduate courses;
- private sector and voluntary sector agencies.

Special access

You may have special access to information from people you know personally. You could try the following:

- friends;
- colleagues;
- your line manager;
- your local quality manager.

We hope you find *lots* of information.

ACTIVITY 3.16

How did you first hear about quality assurance? How did you find out about this book?

- Make a list of ways in which communication about quality assurance in social care could be improved.

- Identify two ways in which you might contribute to the improvement of communication about quality assurance in social care.

You have now completed Part One, Understanding Quality Assurance in Social Care.

Self-Assessment Exercises

Now that you have completed Chapter 3 you may find it helpful to check your progress by trying these self-assessment exercises. You will find our suggested answers at the end of the book.

Exercise 5

Complete the following sentences by choosing a word or phrase from those listed.

1. Quality assurance provides a guarantee that quality will be _____.
   > up to standard
   > high
   > effective
   > cheap

2. One reason why top management should be involved in quality assurance initiatives is that _____.
   > their performance is always poor
   > they know most about it
   > they have power to commit resources to it
   > they have more time for it

3. Professionals should be involved in quality assurance because _____.
   > it helps them to improve their service
   > it helps them to highlight their commitment to consistent high-quality service
   > it helps them to work with other professional groups
   > all of these

4. Quality procedures originated _____ _____.
   > after the Industrial Revolution
   > in the Middle Ages
   > at least as long ago as ancient Egyptian times
   > in Japan

5. The economic success of post-war Japan was partly due to their development of ——— _____techniques.
   > inspection
   > quality assurance
   > craftsmanship
   > quality control

6. Cost-effective quality assurance systems ___ _____.
   > cost a lot
   > cost more than poor-quality service
   > cost less than the costs of poor quality they prevent
   > have no cost implications

Exercise 6

Which of the following statements are true? Write true or false in the space provided.

1. Once standards are set quality has been assured. _____

2. Quality assurance has to be managed.

   _____

3. Quality action is only needed if quality is poor._____

4. There is no government requirement for quality assurance in social care.

   _____

5. Quality procedures developed in manufacturing industry are appropriate for aspects of social care. _____

6. Poor communication can lead to process failure costs. _____

Exercise 7

1. Give two reasons why professionals responsible for setting up quality assurance procedures for the first time should pay particular attention to effective communication.

2. Give two reasons why the Industrial Revolution led to the development of new quality procedures.

3. Give two reasons why poor quality in social care might lead to increased costs.

Exercise 8

Write definitions of the following.

1. inspection;
2. quality assurance;
3. a quality system

Now that you have completed these exercises, check your answers with the solutions at the end of the book.

Assuring quality in social care

Introduction to assuring quality in social care

OBJECTIVES

By the end of Chapter Four you will be able to:

● understand the aims of Part Two;

● Identify quality assurance activities in your own workplace.

Part One introduced you to concepts and definitions underlying quality assurance. It traced the development of quality assurance in industry, health care and social care. You also learned that quality assurance involves setting standards, that quality is everyone's business, and that assessing quality means comparing performance with agreed standards.

In Part Two you will learn how you might take part in quality assurance within your own professional practice.

4.1 Support for quality assurance in social care

In earlier sections (particularly Sections 2.3 (p. 11) and 3.1 (p. 16)) we stressed the importance of involving everyone in quality improvement. We also suggested that it was vitally important to secure a genuine commitment to quality improvement from managers and policy-makers. Ideally, commitment and involvement are expressed by top management in a quality policy which is implemented through setting up a quality system.

A recent study of quality assurance in Social Services Departments (James, 1992) identified five local authorities in which there were established quality assurance systems, and noted that there was a commitment to developing systems in many more. These five authorities had begun to give responsibility for quality assurance to named senior staff. All of them saw the work of their arm's-length inspection units as only one part of their overall quality assurance system. They varied considerably however, in the pattern and aims of their quality activities, and in the way in which professionals and middle managers were involved.

ACTIVITY 4.1

Look back to Section 3.1 where we set out a list of organizational features likely to support quality assurance initiatives. Rate your own area of work by giving a score from 0 to 5 on each of these features (where 0 means that this feature is absent and 5 means that your workplace is as good as it possibly could be with respect to that feature).

FEATURE	SCORE
Accurate and up-to-date documentation	
Effective communication	
Willingness to change	
Training for quality assurance activities	
Commitment from top management	
Commitment from all personnel	
Clear responsibilities for quality activities	

Quality assurance often begins with professionals who are close to the day-to-day activities of care. The success or failure of a quality initiative will obviously be influenced by the support it receives. On the other hand, a successful quality initiative might help to change a previously unsupportive organizational setting.

Many organizations, including some Social Services Departments, have addressed the issue of support for quality assurance by introducing a Total Quality Management programme. These programmes are based on the belief that quality must be integrated into every part of the organization. Different departments can have different approaches to quality assurance, but they all contribute to the organization's overall 'mission' of improving quality. Top management are responsible for setting organization-wide quality goals. They are also responsible for making sure that all departments participate, and for giving quality issues a high profile.

In the rest of this chapter we shall discuss relatively small-scale quality assurance initiatives, which can be undertaken by groups of professionals at any organizational level. We assume a moderately supportive organizational setting, but we make no assumptions about the particular system of quality management.

4.2 The quality cycle

In section 3.1 the stages of the quality assurance cycle were represented in a diagram.

Look again at the diagram. It shows two processes.

1. **Quality appraisal:**
   - setting standards;
   - appraising actual achievement.

2. **Quality action:**
   - planning for improvement;
   - taking action when necessary.

Quality appraisal and quality action are revised in this chapter to guide you through the

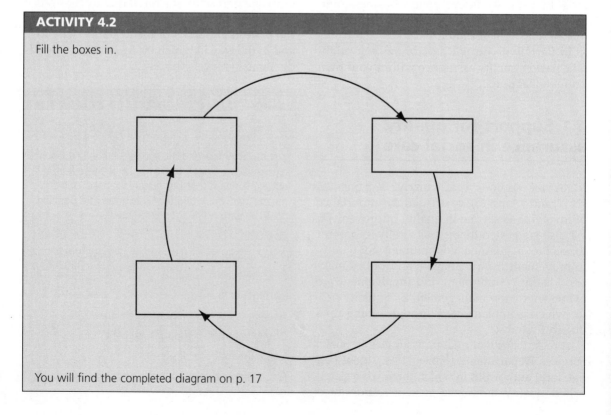

ACTIVITY 4.2

Fill the boxes in.

You will find the completed diagram on p. 17

stages of a full quality assurance initiative. The two halves of the cycle are shown in Figures 4.1 and 4.2, and an overview of the stages in each half follows.

Quality Appraisal

A quality group is established which sets standards, selects appropriate techniques to find out what is happening in practice, and then

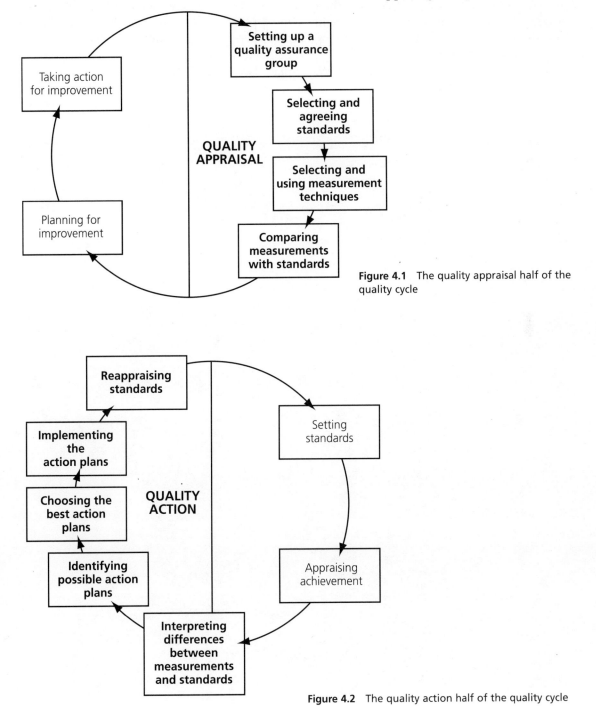

Figure 4.1 The quality appraisal half of the quality cycle

Figure 4.2 The quality action half of the quality cycle

compares observed practice with the agreed standards (see Figure 4.1).

Quality Action

While setting standards and assessing their achievement is interesting, it is of little benefit unless the acquired information is used. Using the information is quality action.

When observed practice is compared with agreed standards, differences may become apparent. Any differences are investigated and action plans are discussed.

Several options for improvement are identified. The quality assurance group chooses the most suitable plan, implements it, and finally reappraises the situation to check that the planned improvements have actually taken place (see Figure 4.2).

Quality appraisal

OBJECTIVES

By the end of Chapter Five you will be able to:

- describe the process of quality appraisal;

- plan for quality appraisal in your own workplace.

To achieve these objectives we shall work through the stages shown in Figure 5.1.

5.1 Setting up a quality assurance group

OBJECTIVES

By the end of this section you will be able to:

- list features which can make quality assurance groups more effective;

- describe procedures for organizing quality assurance groups.

A quality assurance group is a team of people who meet together to undertake quality assurance activities. Working in a group has both advantages and disadvantages. Its advantages lie in bringing together different viewpoints. Its disadvantages have to do with persuading people to work together effectively.

In this section we shall discuss:

- group size;
- group membership;
- group effectiveness;
- organization of meetings.

GROUP SIZE

The ideal group size depends in part on the scope of the intended quality assurance initiative.

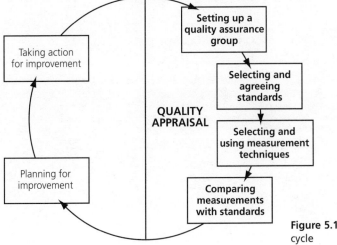

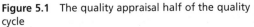

Figure 5.1 The quality appraisal half of the quality cycle

A group with overall responsibility for quality assurance throughout an agency might be large and therefore need to set up subgroups to tackle specific issues. On the other hand, a group considering quality issues in the service delivered in one 'supported accommodation' unit for people with learning disability might involve only two or three people.

There is some evidence to suggest that eight is a good size for a group where the main task is discussion and problem-solving. This size allows a full contribution from individual members.

The rest of this section assumes a quality assurance group with a relatively specific area of responsibility and between four and ten members.

GROUP MEMBERSHIP

Setting up a quality assurance group is like setting up any other work group. Try Activity 5.1 now.

Now look back at your list. You may have included some people primarily because of their position, and others because of their special knowledge or skills. Some may have been included because they are easy to work with.

Check your list again.

- Have you included a client – or a member of a clients' pressure group?
- Have you included all of the people your quality assurance activity might directly affect?
- Have you included someone who has access to negotiation for resources?

GROUP EFFECTIVENESS

You will have had experience of different work groups – care teams, project groups, or informal groups of colleagues. Some will have been more successful than others. Think about your experience and try Activity 5.2 now.

Your experience may or may not be typical, but compare the features that you thought important with those set out by the social psychologist Michael Argyle (Argyle, 1969). He suggests that effective groups have the following features. They:

- meet frequently;
- meet informally as well as formally;
- make jokes and mention personal matters even when they are working;
- have similar attitudes and values;

ACTIVITY 5.1

Think of an aspect of your own work where a quality assurance group might be helpful. Make a list of up to eight people you would like to include as members of your group.

ASPECT OF WORK

NAME   POSITION   REASON FOR INCLUSION

ACTIVITY 5.2

Think of a work group you have been in which was successful in achieving its goals and one which was largely unsuccessful.

Write down some of the features of the effective group and the ineffective group.

EFFECTIVE GROUP   INEFFECTIVE GROUP

- agree upon the purpose of the group;
- have developed an implicit (and sometimes explicit) agreement about who does what in the group;
- include someone who is particularly good at leading discussion;
- have good discussion skills.

Few quality assurance groups will take up this ideal form immediately. It is more likely that effectiveness will begin to emerge after the first two or three meetings. The initiator of the group might help by talking to each member individually to reach agreement on the purpose of the group and to deal with any possible fears or anxieties.

If you are acting as leader of the group, you may need to brush up on skills of facilitating discussion.

- Are you good at summarizing other people's contributions?
- Do you ask contributors to clarify their comments?
- Do you look at other members encouragingly while they speak?
- Are you good at staying quiet while others contribute?
- Do you stop people interrupting each other?
- If people are all talking at once, do you ask them to take turns?

Another matter you may have considered while completing the last activity box is the voluntariness of group membership. One school of thought suggests that quality assurance groups should be made up entirely of volunteers. By definition, volunteers have high levels of commitment. On the other hand, this approach may mean that the people who did not volunteer are the very ones who may not understand or support change. They could obstruct group proposals at a later date. A different approach suggests that quality assurance groups should be 'natural work groups', so that everyone is involved whether they are enthusiasts for change or natural conservatives.

In either of these approaches the quality assurance group may not have representatives from senior levels who can help to authorize change. Humberside Social Services Department set up quality assurance groups by taking a vertical slice through each of their service areas. Each group included senior, middle and first-line managers, relevant professionals, ancillary and support workers, and service users or their representatives.

The approach you choose may depend on more general features of your agency and on its history of innovation and change.

ACTIVITY 5.3

Go back to the quality assurance group membership you suggested earlier in this section. Revise your suggested membership using the following approaches:

● Natural work group

NAME   POSITION

● Vertical slice

NAME   POSITION

ACTIVITY 5.4

Ask your line manager for a view on which approach to group membership would suit your workplace best. Make a note of your manager's reasons for choosing that approach.

ORGANIZATION OF MEETINGS

ACTIVITY 5.5

Think again about your experience of a successful work group. What was it about the way it was run that made it successful? Make a note of your answers.

You may have included some of the following.

● meetings lasted for a fixed period of time;
● a clear agenda was prepared;
● the frequency of meetings was agreed;
● members were informed of the time and

place of meetings, and plenty of notice was given;

- meetings were held away from the immediate workplace, so as to be free from interruption;
- good records were kept of participants at each meeting, decisions made and action to be taken (by whom and by when);
- records were sent to non-group members whose support might be required at a later stage in the initiative.

All of these features help to ensure the smooth and effective operation of a quality assurance group. In health care, the Royal College of Nursing Quality Assurance Network has set up teams of facilitators who have experience of helping groups to run smoothly and effectively. Your own professional organization or agency may also be able to help.

In this section you have considered some aspects of setting up and organizing a quality assurance group. The next stage of the quality cycle involves setting and agreeing standards.

5.2 Setting and agreeing standards

OBJECTIVES

By the end of this section you will be able to:

- choose a topic for standard writing;

- write a standard;

- choose indicators associated with the standard.

Section 2.2 introduced standards, and Section 2.3 discussed who should be involved in setting them.

ACTIVITY 5.6

Go back to Sections 2.2 and 2.3 and read quickly over the main points.

Since standard setting is a key element in any quality assurance initiative, it will be studied in more detail in this section.

There are many different methods of writing standards. The method described in this book has been chosen for its ease and simplicity. Other methods are described in the texts referred to in the relevant 'useful reading' suggested at the end of this book.

Writing a standard involves discussing and agreeing upon:

- a topic;
- a standard statement;
- indicators.

TOPICS

Many quality assurance groups are set up with only a broad idea of the areas in which they might improve quality. A first task is to choose smaller areas within which to begin setting standards and improving quality. Some quality assurance groups have failed as a result of trying to tackle everything at once. Once the group is more experienced it will be possible to return to planning for overall quality.

ACTIVITY 5.7

- Make a list of areas of work in your own agency where it could be helpful to write standards and improve quality.

- Ask a colleague to make a similar list (do not show your colleague your list).

Now compare and discuss your choices.

Perhaps you chose areas where quality is obviously not as good as it might be, or which you and your colleagues would agree are central to your work, or where you thought it would be easy to improve quality quickly.

All of these are sound reasons for choosing areas in which to improve quality.

Norfolk Social Services Department (Cassam and Gupta, 1992) chose areas for quality improvement where there was:

- inexplicable inconsistency in levels of service delivery across the County;
- evidence of consumer dissatisfaction;
- evidence of professional unease regarding service quality;
- a trend in outcomes which ran counter to either Department policy or government targets;
- a key area of activity which had not been reviewed for a long time.

Now go back to your own choices and check whether quality improvement in these areas will be:

- relevant to the aims of your agency – some less successful quality initiatives deal with trivial aspects of service while quality worsens in more central areas;
- easy to achieve – over-ambitious quality initiatives risk demoralizing group members and possibly antagonizing colleagues outside the group;
- acceptable to colleagues – it is always worth consulting widely before beginning quality initiatives;
- demonstrable – new quality assurance groups must be able to demonstrate clearly that they have had an impact on quality;
- yours – while senior management must be fully committed to quality improvement, there is considerable evidence to suggest that quality initiatives 'owned' by staff close to actual service delivery are more likely to be successful.

If your predicted quality improvements have each of these characteristics you are **ready** to begin standard setting on your quality **topic**.

A quality topic is an area of activity or aspect of care for which a quality assurance group has decided to write a standard.

Most quality assurance groups begin by choosing topics which are quite broad. Narrower topics can be identified in most cases. For example, if the topic selected was intake and assessment of new clients, narrower topics might include length of time between initial reception and assessment, written information provided, appropriateness of referral, detail of care plan recording, etc. Thus a range of narrower, more precise topics may be identified from one broad one. The narrower and more precise the topic, the easier it will be to write a standard for it. Topics must be understood and agreed upon by all members of the quality assurance group. Time spent on ensuring this is time well spent.

It is also important to identify the set of clients for whose care the standard is to be written. It could be all users and carers receiving a particular service, or all children on the 'at-risk' register, or all new admissions to a specified residential facility. The standards written should relate to the whole group and be seen as relevant to each member. Standards can be written for large or small groups, or even for individuals.

ACTIVITY 5.8

Go back to one of the areas for quality improvement you worked on in the last two activity boxes. Write down *two* topics from that area and identify a relevant client group for each of them.

Once you have decided on your area for quality improvement and have identified your topic and your client group, you are ready to write a standard statement.

STANDARDS STATEMENTS

In Section 2.2 (p. 7) we noted that standards must:

- be approved or accepted by relevant groups;
- specify what has to be achieved;
- specify the level of achievement required;
- allow for measurement or judgement that the specified level has been achieved.

The standard statement sets down the agreed level of performance appropriate to the client group and relevant to the selected topic.

ACTIVITY 5.9

Choose one of the topics you wrote down in the last activity box. Make a first attempt at writing a standard statement for it.

Standards statements are usually fairly short sentences. A standard statement in the broad area of independent living for older people in residential care, on the topic of telephone access, and developed for all new residents in 'Beechpark' home for older people might be as follows.

- All new residents of 'Beechpark' should have priority access to telephone facilities.

As you may have realized, the quality assurance group agreeing that standard could have problems in trying to judge whether their standard had been met.

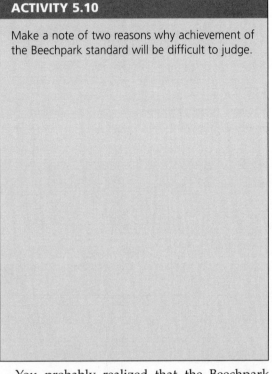

ACTIVITY 5.10

Make a note of two reasons why achievement of the Beechpark standard will be difficult to judge.

You probably realized that the Beechpark standard is not very specific.

- What does 'new' mean? In their first day? Or week? Or month?
- What does 'priority' mean? At any hour of day or night? Or during specified hours? And how long can calls take? Over how far a distance?
- What does 'access' mean? In the residents' own rooms? Down a corridor? Free? At a profit to the agency?

Without a clear and specific answer to these questions, it will not be possible to judge whether or not the quality of care is at the required standard. The standard will not **indicate** when it has been achieved.

INDICATORS

Indicators specify clearly and precisely the levels of performance which have to be achieved in order to satisfy the standard. When the standard has been satisfied there is a clear indication of it.

ACTIVITY 5.11

Make a list of the indicators you think would help you to be sure that the telephone access standard had been met. (You will find it helpful to ask yourself the questions 'What do we mean?' And 'How do we know?' about each part of the standard.)

Go back to your own standard from the earlier activity box. Rewrite it as clearly as you can. Make a list of the indicators that would be helpful.

You have now written clear and specific standards and have chosen indicators related to them. It should be easy to make judgements or to take measurements which will convince you (or other observers) that your standards have or have not been satisfied.

Now go back to your final version of the telephone access standard. How much access did you let your residents have? You probably noticed that you could have set a perfectly clear and specific standard indicating that residents should have constant access. On the other hand, you could have written a perfectly clear and specific standard indicating that residents should have only one 3-minute call in their first month. Making judgements about the level of service it is reasonable to expect represents one of the most important functions of a quality assurance group. It is also a reason why it is important to think carefully about the membership of the group, and about its relationship to other groups making routine management and resource decisions.

The levels of service quality that individual quality assurance groups decide on are determined by many factors. Resources are important, but so are users', managers' and professionals' perceptions of the situation. The ingenuity of the group and the time they devote to trying to work out ways of improving the level of service quality achievable within existing or obtainable resources should make a significant contribution. Investigations of poor-quality service often reveal groups of professionals who say they had known quality was poor, but that they never had time to think of ways of improving it. They may also have thought that they were the only people who were concerned. Quality assurance groups reduce professional isolation.

ACTIVITY 5.12

Go back to your own standard from the last activity box. Revise it in the light of your knowledge of what could reasonably be achieved within current resources.

In Section 2.2 (p. 7) we referred to Donabedian's work on quality assurance standards. He suggests that standards can be set for three aspects of care:

- structure;
- process;
- outcome.

Often structure, process and outcome *indicators* can be established for one standard.

On this occasion, let us assume a standard has been set for the quality of meals in the Beechpark residential home.

Structure

Structure indicators specify the level of resource provision needed for achievement of a standard. In our meals example, structure indicators could refer to budget for purchase of foodstuffs, number and grades of kitchen staff, or kitchen accommodation and equipment.

Process

Process indicators specify the activities which must be undertaken to achieve the standard. They are the 'doing' part of the standard. They state who must do what, to whom, when and how, in order to achieve the standard. In the meals example, these indicators could refer to time taken to bring meals from kitchen to table, to the attentiveness of the serving staff, or to residents' involvement in the choice of menu.

Outcome

Outcome indicators specify the end results of care. As noted in earlier sections, they can be short term or long term. In the meals example, short-term outcome indicators might include temperature of food served, variety of meals in a given time period, or availability of varied vegetarian or other special options. Longer-term outcome indicators might include residents' overall satisfaction with the meals provided, low (or no) incidence of food-related illness, or residents' adherence to special diets.

Commonly used outcome indicators in social care include:

- client satisfaction;
- client knowledge;
- change in client attitudes;
- change in client function;
- low levels of return for further or repeated service.

ACTIVITY 5.13

Consider the following two outcome indicators.

- All residents express satisfaction with the meals provided.

- No menu main course should appear more than twice in one week.

Which is easier to use?

We think that the second indicator is easier to use. It is more precise and more easily agreed upon. The first one is less precise – how do you know when the client is 'satisfied'? Many indicators of social care quality are changes in people's attitudes or opinions. They cannot be observed and measured directly. We shall return to measurement of these indicators in the next section of this book.

Some quality assurance groups use forms for writing standards and specifying indicators. They often also include a note of who is responsible for maintaining the standard, and of the dates of appraisal and reappraisal. A typical form is shown in Figure 5.2.

ACTIVITY 5.14

● Go back to your own standard from the earlier activity boxes.

● Write one structure, one process and one outcome indicator for it.

A great many indicator statements can be written for any one standard. Quality assurance groups have to choose indicators which are both relevant to standards and easy to use. They must be **SMART** indicators:

● **S**pecific;
● **M**easurable;
● **A**chievable;
● **R**elevant;
● **T**argeted.

Specific

An indicator statement must be clearly understood by everyone who uses it. The more specific it is, the easier it will be to understand.

Measurable

Some indicator statements lead to straightforward 'yes' or 'no' judgements. Beechpark residents might either have or not have a telephone in their rooms. Other indicators might require measurement. Residents might need to have

Topic:					Appraisal date:	
Subtopic:					Authorized by:	
Relevant clients:						
Standard statement:						
No.	Structure indicator	No.	Process indicator	No.	Outcome indicator	

Figure 5.2 A standard document

access to a telephone a certain number of metres from their room, or access to it during a certain number of hours per day. Many social care standards refer to changes in attitudes or values. They cannot be observed or measured directly. 'Respect for clients', for example, cannot be seen or heard directly, but it is not too difficult to think of behaviour which would indicate its presence or absence. Standards statements may not be expressed in measurable terms, but indicator statements must be. Without some form of measurability it will not be possible to agree with confidence that the required level of service quality has been achieved.

Achievable

Quality assurance groups must choose between ambition and realism. If they set over-ambitious standards with unrealistic indicators they may worry and even antagonize colleagues who are not group members. They are also likely to become disappointed when their achievements do not match their ambitions. It is better to begin carefully by planning and achieving small-scale quality improvements. Publicity for small but demonstrable early achievements can lead to greater things.

Relevant

Quality assurance groups generally begin with broad standards statements. They then select narrower topics and move from there to a choice of indicators which are specific, measurable and achievable. With each of these choices they run the risk of moving too far from the intentions of the original standard. Indicator statements can be very specific but not relevant to the standard. The danger is most marked where the original standard is for something not directly observable – such as respect for clients, or client satisfaction with service. It is worth reviewing indicator statements occasionally to be sure that, taken together, they look likely to provide a reasonable assessment of the original standard.

We all agreed accommodation quality had to be improved – it was just a pity we couldn't get the funding for the second half of the plan.

Targeted

Indicator statements must include a clear statement of the group of clients or aspect of service to which they will apply. Standards and indicators developed for one group of clients are sometimes 'lifted' to save time in developing new ones for other apparently similar groups. This can present problems if the description of the original target group is unclear.

In this section you have chosen topics for standard writing, written standards and chosen indicators.

Look back at the quality cycle in Figure 5.1 (p. 37). You have now completed the first two stages of quality appraisal – setting up your quality assurance group, and setting and agreeing standards. You are ready for the next stage – selecting and using measurement techniques.

5.3 Selecting and using measurement techniques

OBJECTIVES

By the end of this section you will be able to:

- describe some techniques available for measuring the achievement of standards;

- list some advantages and disadvantages of each of these techniques;

- consider which techniques might be appropriate in different contexts.

When setting standards and selecting techniques it is important to consider when and how they will be monitored. You saw in the last section that the achievement of some indicators was very easy to observe. A simple check-list may be all that is needed if all of a standard's indicators lead to a yes/no assessment. Other indicators may require sophisticated measurement techniques.

Standards can be appraised after or during the delivery of care. These techniques are often referred to as *retrospective* and *concurrent* appraisal, respectively.

Retrospective appraisal usually includes some combination of the following:

- audit;
- interviews;
- questionnaires;
- focus groups.

Concurrent appraisal includes all of the above with the addition of:

- direct observation.

We shall now consider each of these techniques.

AUDIT

The word audit is sometimes thought to be another term for quality assurance. Quality assurance in hospitals is often described as 'medical audit' or 'clinical audit'. More accurately, audit means scrutinizing records. Financial audit means checking accounts to be sure that they have been properly kept. In health care and social care, audit means examining patients' or clients' records for evidence of care quality.

You may have included records of assessments, care plans and case reviews.

Audit of records allows rapid appraisal of quality delivered to relatively large numbers of clients. In hospitals in the USA, records clerks go through patient records looking for agreed signs of possible poor quality (incomplete records, secondary infections, unanticipated death, etc). These patients' cases are then reviewed in detail by teams of clinicians. Norfolk Social Services Department carried out an audit of the work done by area fieldwork teams (Cassam and Gupta, 1992). The audit team looked at all referrals coming into each fieldwork office over a set period, and selected the case files of the last six children and the last six adults admitted to care for detailed examination. They also examined a sample of each fieldworker's case files and looked at how time and work were organized.

Audit appraisals are based on records. They are therefore only as good as the records themselves. If records are poor or incomplete, then the appraisal of care quality will be inaccurate. It will also be inaccurate if the sample of records examined is biased or unusual in some way. Finally, people involved in keeping records can get very good at doing just that. Sometimes, perfect records are produced which bear little relationship to the standard of care provided. This is particularly likely if the staff concerned know that care quality will be appraised through audit. Care may even deteriorate because too much time is devoted to the completion of the records.

ACTIVITY 5.17

Go back to the list of available records you drew up in the last activity box.

Make a note of the advantages and disadvantages of appraising quality by referring to these records.

Check whether you included the following.

Advantages

- Records are usually readily available.
- Establishment of record-based audit encourages good record-keeping.
- Records are available for a long period.

Disadvantages

- Assessment based on poor records will be inaccurate.
- Care must be taken to examine a representative sample of records.
- Excessive time spent on record-keeping decreases the time available for care.

INTERVIEWS

The records we considered in the previous section are written records. Much information about service quality is never written down.

The majority of clients, for example, never have an opportunity to write down what they think of the service they are receiving. One way of gaining access to this store of information is to talk to people. Interviews are a systematic way of talking to people.

ACTIVITY 5.18

Make a list of people who might have information about service quality in your own workplace.

You probably included service users and their carers, but did you also include your colleagues, your managers, colleagues from referring agencies, or people assessed but refused service?

An evaluation of managed domiciliary care schemes in Northern Ireland involved interviews with users, carers, scheme staff, scheme managers and senior managers (Whittington *et al.*, 1994).

Both clients and colleagues can find answering questions face to face easier and less time-consuming than providing written answers.

Depending on the type of information being looked for, interviews can be:

- structured;
- unstructured;
- semi-structured.

Semi-structured interviews include a mixture of structured and unstructured sections. Structured interviews have pre-set questions. The range of possible answers is usually fixed in advance, and the interviewer has only to tick boxes corresponding to the answers given.

Returning to the meals example, a few structured questions may be all that is needed. For example:

> 'Did you get a chance to choose what you wanted to eat?
> Please answer yes or no'.

and

> 'How many choices were there?
> Please give a number'.

If these questions are repeated for each main meal, then the indicators for the standard have been assessed. In a structured situation, the interviewer's role is mainly to reassure the interviewee and to make sure that they understand the questions and answer them clearly.

The interviewer has a larger role to play when interviews are unstructured. In an unstructured interview the interviewer has a clear idea of the areas to be covered, but leaves more room for the interviewee to put responses in a personal context. Answers are less predictable. One danger of unstructured interviews is that interviewers may unintentionally influence interviewees' answers, or distort them in writing them down.

In the meals example, questions could begin with the following question:

> 'Did you enjoy your meals?'

It would be up to the interviewer to use subsequent probing comments, such as:

> 'Really – why was that?'

or

> 'I see – tell me more.'

This would uncover the importance and reality of choice for that particular individual. The structured interview might never discover that, although there was a varied menu, choices were exclusively between the dull and the disgusting. Even a semi-structured interview with the final question

> *'Is there anything else you would like to say about the food?'*

would reveal such a state of affairs.

If the standards being appraised are relevant to a large client group, a series of decisions must be made about who is to be interviewed. Any source of consistent bias must be avoided. It would be unwise, for example, to interview only male clients or only clients dealing with one particular member of staff.

Interviewers who are known to clients may be able to persuade them to talk freely and to give specific and relevant detail. Their major disadvantage is that clients who have negative opinions may hold back for fear of giving offence. Many quality assurance initiatives have been criticized for assessing clients' satisfaction with service provided while they were still receiving the service – in that context an interview can seem like blackmail. Colleagues, too, can be difficult to convince of the confidentiality of negative comments.

In summary, advantages and disadvantages of interviews as a way of finding out about service quality include the following.

Advantages

- Interviewers can make sure that questions are understood and answers clearly given.
- Interviewees who would find giving written information difficult (or too time consuming) may be able to provide information face to face.
- Interviewees have an opportunity to raise issues that may have been missed in designing the interview.
- In unstructured interviews, interviewers can explore attitudes and opinions in depth, and can respond to interviewees' appearance and other non-verbal cues.

Disadvantages

- The interviewer may unconsciously influence the answers given.
- Interviewees can find it difficult to express negative opinions in a face-to-face situation.
- It can be difficult to arrange convenient times for interviews.
- Interviews are time-consuming and therefore costly.

QUESTIONNAIRES

Questionnaires, like interviews, can be structured or unstructured. Structured questions (usually called closed questions) are relatively narrow and precise. They have a fixed number of pre-set answers from which respondents select a response. Unstructured or open-ended questions are broader, and allow respondents to write in their answers in their own way.

Questionnaires are used very frequently in quality assurance. They are particularly popular as a way of obtaining customers' or clients' views on quality. In 1989, Norfolk Social Services Department carried out a comprehensive study of meals in residential homes in which 437 residents completed a questionnaire on the quality of the food (Cassam and Gupta, 1992).

Questionnaire construction is not difficult, but there are pitfalls which must be avoided. Questions must be clear and easy to understand, the questionnaire should not be so long that respondents are put off filling it in, and the range of questions must cover the main aspects of the topic being investigated. There are many helpful books on questionnaire construction. We have listed some in the 'useful reading' section at the end of this book.

Questionnaires can be administered either by sending them to people by mail, or by asking groups to complete them together at a particular place and time. The second method has two advantages. First, there is an opportunity for clarification of questions and for helping respondents with their answers. However, the main advantage is that there is more chance of a large proportion of respondents completing the questionnaire. Sending questionnaires by post can involve two or even three reminder mailings before a large enough number of completed questionnaires is received.

The general advantages and disadvantages of questionnaire use are well known. They include the following.

Advantages

- They can be administered easily to large groups.
- They are economical in time and money.
- Each recipient is asked the same questions.
- Interviewer bias is eliminated.

Disadvantages

- The response rate can be low.
- Some kinds of clients (and professionals) are less likely to respond to questionnaires than others.
- Questionnaires are inappropriate for people who have language difficulties or problems with written material.
- Questionnaires may not be completed by the intended respondents but by others who may have different views.

ACTIVITY 5.19

Think of (or look back at) a feedback questionnaire you have recently been asked to complete.

- How could it have been improved?

- What were its best features?

That's it Mr Smith – you tick the box that says you are entirely satisfied with the quality of my care – that one there.

● What were its worst features?

FOCUS GROUPS

A relatively new way of testing opinion regarding service quality is the use of focus groups. A focus group is a small group of individuals (usually between 6 and 12) selected for their relevance to the area of investigation. In social care quality assurance they might be selected from client records and could involve clients, carers, etc. On other occasions they could be groups of staff associated with a particular area of service (possibly dealing with some aspect of internal quality, such as communication, referral times or records systems). The group meets in a comfortable environment (preferably not where service was delivered) for a period of at least 1 hour. Client groups are usually paid for out-of-pocket expenses. Members of the group are assured of confidentiality, and are told the aim of the quality initiative. Discussion is facilitated by a group 'moderator' who is usually a member of the quality assurance team which has set up the initiative. It is sometimes helpful to have a second team member present to help with practicalities.

Discussion can be very open, with the moderator only introducing the topic in a general way and asking the group members for their views. Moderators sometimes find it helpful to

have a list of sub-topics which they introduce one by one as discussion progresses. Focus groups are deliberately relatively lengthy so that groups can relax into full and frank exploration of their views. Moderators often say very little, but can help to steer the discussion to make sure that everyone has an opportunity to contribute, and that all views are represented. The discussion is tape-recorded and a written version is then transcribed. The transcript is usually analysed by the moderator(s) who were present at the actual discussion.

The advantages and disadvantages of focus groups include the following.

Advantages

● Group members are free to contribute their views and to raise issues which are important to them.
● Issues are explored in some depth.
● New issues can be raised.
● Group members share their ideas and refine their opinions in the course of the group.

Disadvantages

● Getting the group together in a comfortable location is both time-consuming and costly.
● The groups selected may not properly represent the relevant staff or client group.
● Group discussion may be dominated by a few talkative members.
● Groups may tend to 'go along' with the views of a few apparently authoritative members.
● Interpretation of the transcript of discussion may be biased or distorted.

ACTIVITY 5.20

Think of a quality issue in your own workplace where focus groups could produce valuable views.

● What kind of people would you invite to become group members?

● How would you select them?

DIRECT OBSERVATION

All of the methods we have considered so far involve reconstruction of episodes of care or aspects of service delivery *after they have happened*. Records and memories may be biased or inaccurate, and the quality appraisal based on them may therefore not be valid or fair. Direct observation avoids some of the difficulties associated with reconstructing events from records or memory. It may also be the only way to 'catch' the detail of care.

Who the observers are is important. Direct observation of some aspects of social care can be difficult for people without sufficient specialist knowledge. On the other hand, a regular participant in a specialist group of social care professionals may miss or even distort significant events. This is because they think they know what they are going to see, and they therefore forget to look.

Confidentiality is an issue in all aspects of social care quality appraisal. It is particularly important if care delivery itself is to be observed. There may be some particularly sensitive areas of social care where the presence of anyone other than the client and the professional may not be possible at all.

Observers must:

● be acceptable to those to be observed;
● be as unobtrusive as possible;
● have sufficient background knowledge to understand what is going on;

● be able to maintain some degree of objectivity.

Some quality assurance systems solve the problem of selecting observers by having groups of similar units or services undergoing observation during the same period. Staff from each unit are then involved as observers of the other units. When the results are pooled, staff from each unit have been both observed and observer. They are then better able to share their experiences and to produce something approaching an accurate and useful record.

ACTIVITY 5.21

● Next time you have coffee with friends or colleagues, agree that you and one other person will make a record of everything that happens in a specified 5-minute period of conversation.

● Compare and discuss your records.

You probably faced some problems in this activity. First, your colleagues may have decided they would rather not be observed. Even if they agreed, their behaviour may have been subtly (or not so subtly!) artificial. This is the major difficulty in direct observation. The behaviour of observed people is changed if they are aware of being the subject of attention. In the quality assurance context, colleagues who are being observed will be tempted to be 'on their best behaviour'.

A further problem which can be encountered in direct observation is not being able to keep pace with events. As notes are made about one event, another is unfolding, and records may be incomplete. Records and transcripts can be re-examined and interview questions or even questionnaire completion can be repeated. Direct observation has to be accurate first time. Some of these difficulties can be resolved if quality indicators are carefully specified so that the observer has specific events to monitor. If indicators are precisely specified they can be rephrased into questions which can be answered 'yes' or 'no' or 'not applicable'. A number of precise indicators can be combined into a check-list. Observers should have clear guidelines as to how often observations are to be made or check-lists to be ticked.

The advantages and disadvantages of direct observation include the following.

Advantages

- Immediacy.
- Lack of retrospective bias.

Disadvantages

- Introduction of artificiality.
- Observer bias due to ignorance.
- Observer bias due to over-involvement.
- Possible incompleteness of recording.
- Possible inaccuracy of recording.

Sampling

All of the techniques we have discussed require some element of sampling.

- How many records are to be examined? Which ones?
- How many clients are to be interviewed? Who should they be?
- How many questionnaires are to be sent? To whom?
- Who should the members of focus groups be?
- How many colleagues are to be observed? Who should they be?

Issues of sampling are discussed in detail in some of the referenced texts, but there are two main rules.

1. The sample selected must be unbiased – it must be as like the whole group as it can be.
2. The sample must yield measurements in a quantity which the group can realistically handle – there is no point in administering a large number of lengthy questionnaires if it will take 18 months to analyse the answers.

These two rules of sampling are at odds with each other. The representativeness rule might suggest a large sample (or even 100 per cent inclusion), but the practicality rule suggests a small one. The quality assurance group decides on the balance. The group might consult someone who is experienced in this area.

Systems for appraising standards

One way to ease the problems of measurement might be to use a measurement technique which someone else has devised and used successfully in a context similar to your own.

In health care, a number of 'off-the-shelf' techniques for appraising quality have become available. Some could be adapted for use in social care. They include systems based on direct observation of care and systems based on audit of records of care. The list of useful reading at the end of this book includes several texts which give details.

ACTIVITY 5.22

Ask your line manager if any quality appraisal techniques have been regularly used in your workplace, or in similar settings.

Choosing and piloting measurement techniques

All of the techniques you have now studied have both advantages and disadvantages. Your quality assurance group will have to choose which of them are best for the appraisal of the standards they are working on. The group may find it helpful to check with colleagues who have more experience of measurement and appraisal of standards. Whichever technique you choose, it will be advisable to try it out on a few people or records before using it in the real context. This is called *piloting* your measurement technique. Even very experienced quality assessors pilot and modify their measurement techniques before actually using them.

It can sometimes be best to use a combination of techniques. Birmingham Social Services Department undertook an audit of care provided in about half of the city's residential homes (James 1992). Using standards developed from 'Homes are for Living In' (Department of Health, 1989) and other local and national documents, pairs of auditors appraised the quality of care. Their appraisal was based on direct observation, interviews with staff, residents and relatives, and an examination of records.

Focus groups in particular are often used in combination with interview or postal questionnaire surveys of larger groups. They are used before the larger survey to help to identify useful questions and areas to be explored. They can then be used again after the survey to discuss its results and to make sure that they are being interpreted sensibly.

In this section we have considered ways of measuring the extent to which quality standards have been met. Quality assurance groups must bear issues of measurement in mind throughout the process of determining quality topics, standards and indicators.

The next stage of quality appraisal involves comparing the measurements obtained with the standards set and indicators identified.

5.4 Comparing measurements with standards

OBJECTIVES

By the end of this section you will be able to:

- outline the steps involved in comparing measurements with indicators and standards;

- decide when measurements should be compared with standards;

- decide who should be involved in making the comparison;

- identify potential difficulties in carrying out the comparison;

- suggest ways of avoiding these difficulties.

COMPARING MEASUREMENTS WITH INDICATORS AND STANDARDS

The earlier stages of the quality cycle, which were discussed in earlier sections, are as follows:

- choosing an area for quality improvement;
- choosing a quality topic;
- writing a standard statement;
- choosing indicators associated with the standard;
- deciding what kinds of indicators are to be measured – structure (S), process (P), or outcome (O);
- deciding by what date the standard is to have been appraised;
- deciding who is responsible for the appraisal;
- deciding which type of appraisal is to be performed – concurrent or retrospective;
- deciding how each indicator is to be measured – which measurement technique will be used and who or what will be subject to measurement;

- carrying out the measurement.

In some quality assurance systems comparison of measurements with indicators and standards is assisted by documenting information in a structured form. One simple version is set out in Figure 5.3.

The information from the initial stages of appraisal is written on the form. The selected indicators are reworded as questions and written in the second column. Space is allowed on the form for comments. It is useful to know about any 'odd' occurrences. The assessor decides whether the standard has been satisfactorily met, and notes the decision at the bottom of the form. The decision is simple if all indicator questions have clear positive or clear negative answers. However, this is not always the case.

Consider the results from our earlier telephone access example set out in Figure 5.4.

A decision is now necessary as to how important each of the indicators is in deciding whether the standard can be judged to be 'satisfied' or not. Also, will there be a 'margin' in which a standard could be judged to be satisfied, although some of the indicators fall slightly short of the specified level?

These are decisions which may need the whole quality assurance group's judgement. It may even be useful to involve other people.

WHO SHOULD BE INVOLVED IN COMPARING MEASUREMENTS WITH STANDARDS?

In many cases the quality assurance group which sets standards also compares its measurements with them. However, this is not

Topic:			Appraisal date:		
Subtopic			Person responsible:		
Client group and sample size:					
Standard statement:					
S/P/O No.	Indicator	Measurement technique	% Achievement	Assessor signature	

COMMENTS:

SIGNED: DATE:
Appraiser responsible:

Figure 5.3 Appraisal form

Topic: Contact with family and friends		Appraisal date: 3.2.97		
Subtopic: Telephone access		Person responsible: Jane Bloggs		
Client group and sample size: All residents. 50% sample i.e. 27				
Standard statement: All residents will have easy access to a payphone between 10.00 a.m. and 10.00 p.m.				
S/P/O No.	Indicator	Measurement technique	% Achievement	Assessor signature
S1	Payphone installed on each landing	Observation	100%	*MSmith*
S2	Payphone switched on and working at set times	Observation at intervals over 1 week	100%	*MSmith*
P1	Care assistants talk to all residents about possibility of calls	Interviews with sample residents	52% (14)	*JBloggs*
P2	Care assistants help residents who have difficulty using telephones	Interviews with sample residents	80% of those with difficulty (4)	*JBloggs*
O1	Residents report satisfaction with telephone access	Interviews with sample residents	93% (25)	*JBloggs*
O2	All residents make at least one call per week	Observation over 3 weeks and interviews with sample residents	56% (15)	*MSmith*
COMMENTS: 1. One resident suggests special apparatus for people who are hard of hearing 2. O2 Observations were unreliable as care assistants did not want to 'police' telephones, and on the other hand care assistants think one resident claimed she had made calls when she hadn't.				
SIGNED: *Jane Bloggs* Appraiser responsible		DATE: 3.2.97		

Figure 5.4 A completed appraisal form

always the best procedure. Some other suggestions are made below.

Those who wrote the standard

Advantages

- Detailed knowledge of the standard and its context.

Disadvantages

- Possible bias due to closeness to the situation.
- Possible bias due to vested interests.

Managers with responsibility in the area

Advantages

- Wider perspective.
- Probable involvement in eventual quality action.

Disadvantages

- Bias due to conflicting priorities.
- Intimidating to more junior members of the quality assurance group.

Colleagues from a similar setting

Advantages

- Professional background which permits understanding of the standard.
- Usually have no vested interests.
- Acceptable to all members of the quality assurance group.

Disadvantages

- Bias in favour of colleagues with whom they have a close identification.

WHEN SHOULD MEASUREMENTS BE COMPARED WITH STANDARDS?

It takes time to appraise standards thoroughly, and it would be time-consuming, if not impossible, to appraise every standard on every possible occasion. Quality assurance groups have to decide when each standard is to be appraised, and which aspects of it are to be appraised on a given occasion. If standards are being appraised as part of an overall quality assurance system, there may be clear guidelines on scheduling appraisals. If not, the quality assurance group will have to agree upon a system of its own.

ACTIVITY 5.23

Think of a standard which could be set in your own workplace (or go back to the one you wrote in Section 5.2). Now answer the following questions.

- How much would quality be likely to vary in this area?

Figure 5.7   That's the quality appraisal group in there. They don't get out much.

- How often would quality be likely to vary in this area?

- How easy would it be to check quality by appraising the standard?

- How often would it be sensible to check quality by appraising the standard?

You probably found that your answer to the last question was influenced by your answers to the other three. Scheduling appraisals so that quality is maintained and improved where possible is not always simple. Quality assurance groups also have to bear in mind that quality

action and improvement are their real aims. The second half of the quality cycle requires its own time and effort. Quality appraisal for its own sake or because the group are very proud of their carefully thought out standards and measuring techniques wastes both time and resources.

There are two main ways to schedule the appraisal of standards:

- according to a plan;
- as problems emerge.

Planned schedules could involve appraising every standard within a specified period, or appraising them in a specified order taking as long as is required for each one – or some combination of these.

Problem-centred scheduling can mean simply waiting for areas of poor quality to become noticeably so, or it can mean regular screening of an area of practice to pick out areas where more detailed appraisal would be helpful. In a variation on this system, *outcome standards* only are appraised on a set schedule. *Structure* and *process* standards are only appraised if outcome standards are not being met.

ACTIVITY 5.24

Identify the following.

- An area of activity in your own workplace which would benefit from regular fixed period appraisal of all standards.

- An area of activity in your own workplace which would benefit from appraisal of standards using a screening procedure.

Screening systems are relatively economical and ensure that poor quality does not go unnoticed. However, they have some disadvantages. Looking for poor outcome quality only could lead to a group missing a situation where care could be improved if process and structure criteria were appraised. It is possible that care outcomes are good despite inadequate structure and process quality. It is also possible that quality care is being achieved at a higher cost than is necessary. A further disadvantage is the negative focus of screening. Quality assurance systems that never highlight excellent or more than adequate quality can seem punitive and demoralizing. This can make it difficult to ensure that appraisal is followed by quality action. It is also rather depressing for the quality assurance group itself.

Once dates are set for appraisal, it is usual to make them widely known. This lets people who will be involved or affected plan accordingly. However, it also allows time for 'polishing doorknobs' so that quality will appear better than it really is. This is partly offset by the benefits of thinking through what is involved in 'appearing better'!

DIFFICULTIES IN COMPARING MEASUREMENTS WITH STANDARDS

ACTIVITY 5.25

Make a list of possible difficulties involved in comparing measurements with standards.

There should be little or no difficulty in comparing measurements with standards if:

- standards are appropriate;
- indicators are a precise index of standards;
- methods of measurement are appropriate;
- measurement techniques have been used accurately;
- contexts of measurement have been taken into account.

Despite all of this, there will always be a judgement to be made in going from the measurements taken to the conclusions which can justifiably be drawn from them. You only have to consider the different interpretations which politicians of opposing parties place on the same figures to realize that there are difficulties in going beyond the word 'therefore'.

In these sections you have considered one approach to the appraisal of standards.

You have now completed the first half of the quality cycle.

Self-Assessment Exercises

Now that you have completed Chapters 4 and 5 you may find it helpful to check your progress by trying these self-assessment exercises. You will find our suggested answers at the end of the book.

Exercise 9

Complete the following sentences by choosing a word or phrase from those listed.

1. Good group leaders _____.
    never make jokes
    know more about the topic being discussed than other group members
    are good at summarizing other people's contributions
    have loud voices

2. The more specific a quality topic, is the ____ _____.
    harder it is to measure
    easier it will be to write a standard for it
    the more likely it is to lead to reduced costs
    the more trivial it is

3. A quality indicator specifies _____ _____.
    the level of performance required to satisfy a standard
    who should be involved in quality action
    how achievement should be measured
    the quality action required

4. A particular disadvantage of records-based audit is that it _____.
    is complicated to undertake
    is only possible for small groups of patients
    can lead to too much attention being paid to records for their own sake
    can lead to patient complaints

5. Semi-structured questionnaires _____ _____.
    contain open questions only
    can only be administered by post
    contain a mix of open and closed questions
    can only be administered face to face with respondents

6. Screening procedures are most often used in quality assurance to _____.
    select members of quality assurance groups
    make sure quality action takes place
    identify instances of poor quality for more detailed investigation and review
    identify and reward the highest quality

Exercise 10

Which of the following statements are true? Write true or false in the space provided.

1. Quality assurance groups should be made up entirely of volunteers. _____

2. A group facilitator is someone who helps the group to run smoothly. _____

3. The first quality topic a group chooses should always be in the area of poorest quality. _____

4. Direct observation is often used as part of retrospective audit. _____

5. Focus group discussion is tightly controlled by the group moderator. _____.

6. One of the most important rules in selecting a sample of cases for review is that the group of cases selected should be as much like the whole group as possible. _____.

Exercise 11

1. Give two reasons why some groups might be more effective than others.

2. Give two reasons why poor choice of quality indicators might lead to difficulty in improving quality.

3. Give two reasons for deciding to use a postal questionnaire as part of a quality initiative in social care.

Exercise 12

1. Outline the stages of quality appraisal.

2. Identify five important features of an effective quality indicator.

3. Identify two advantages and two disadvantages of using interviews as part of quality appraisal.

Now that you have completed these exercises, check your answers with the solutions at the end of the book.

6 Quality action

OBJECTIVES

By the end of Chapter Six you will be able to:

● describe each of the stages in the action half of the quality cycle;

● discuss review of standards.

You will remember from Section 4.2 (p. 34) that there were five stages in the quality action half of the quality cycle.

6.1 Identifying reasons for differences between measurements and standards

OBJECTIVES

By the end of this section you will be able to:

● identify possible reasons for gaps between performance measures and standards;

● comment on quality assurance group membership for the quality action phase;

● discuss the importance of good communication in the quality action phase.

When all the stages of quality appraisal are complete, the quality assurance group is ready to tackle quality action. This is an essential part of quality assurance. There is no point in collecting information if it is not used to initiate action to improve the quality of care.

Action is planned in response to the comparison of observed practice with a standard. As you learned in the last section, standards are difficult to set with precision and measurement is imperfect, so it is prudent to consider all measurements carefully before any action is discussed. Were the measures really valid, or were there special circumstances which affected the results? If there is any doubt, it may be necessary to reappraise the standard.

Once the measurements are considered to be sound, the process of quality action can begin. The quality assurance group is faced with two possible situations for each standard appraised:

● observed performance meets or exceeds the standard;
● observed performance falls short of the standard.

In either case the quality assurance group will want to discuss the results.

ACTIVITY 6.1

Consider the performance of these two quality assurance groups.

● Group A

Group A sets standards and appraises them carefully. Almost all performance measures meet the standards set. Quality action consists of identifying a few measures for quality improvement, one of which also reduces the costs of service delivery.

● Group B

Group B sets standards and appraises them carefully. Many performance measures indicate that

Figure 6.1 The quality action half of the quality cycle.

standards are not being met. Quality action consists of initiating a number of new procedures and setting dates for reappraisal of standards. In one case substantial additional resources will be required.

Which quality assurance group is doing the best job?

You probably thought that both groups were doing a good job but in different ways. Also, they may have been working in rather different circumstances. Group A may want to look back at their standards to see whether they are artificially low. If not, they are in the lucky position of being able to congratulate their colleagues and to publicize the achievement throughout the agency. They can then go forward to improved quality in that positive spirit. Group B may have set slightly unrealistic standards and run the risk of being unable to sustain

morale through the difficult process of improvement.

OBSERVED PRACTICE MEETS OR EXCEEDS THE STANDARD

After the congratulations have taken place, the group must look for information to help in the process of continuous quality improvement.

- Has observed practice consistently met or exceeded the standard on previous appraisals? If so perhaps the standard should be placed at a higher level.
- Has performance improved since previous appraisals? If so, what changes have been made to procedures and/or resources that could account for it? Should similar changes be made in related areas of activity?
- Could colleagues from the high standards area offer guidance or training to colleagues in similar areas where performance is at a lower standard?
- Are service users easier to work with in some way in the high standards area? If they are,

does this mean that users in more 'difficult' areas need different procedures or additional resources?

ACTIVITY 6.2

● Think of an area of activity in your own workplace where you think service quality is particularly good.

● List three ways in which it could be improved.

There is always room for improvement.

MEASURED PERFORMANCE FALLS SHORT OF THE STANDARD

Goodwill and commitment to quality improvement are very important when measured performance falls short of the standard. This is the point at which time devoted to obtaining top management commitment, keeping communication channels open with relevant colleagues and careful selection of group members will pay off.

ACTIVITY 6.3

Imagine there has been a quality improvement initiative in your own workplace. Standards have been set and appraised. You were involved in standard setting and agreed that the standards set and indicators specified were all quite reasonable. Performance has now been appraised, and it has turned out that service quality is below standard in the area of work for which you are responsible.

The following scenarios illustrate different approaches to this problem. Which would you prefer? And why?

● Scenario A

A letter is sent to you (and a copy to your line manager). The letter goes into great detail about the value of quality assurance before pointing out that 'quality in your own and other areas had an average compliance rating of only 27 per cent. This will be the focus of discussion at a future meeting of the quality management liaison group'. The letter is clearly a standard letter and one or two of your colleagues also seem to have received it. You are not sure who has and who has not.

● Scenario B

It has been made clear throughout the standard setting and appraisal exercise that you and your colleagues would be involved in discussing the results of the exercise. At various points in the measurement phase you have been asked to comment on the way in which measurements are being collected and interpreted. You are not in the quality assurance group yourself, but you are on good terms with one of the members and hear what is happening. You have had a date in your diary for some time for a 'quality feedback' meeting. A week or so before the meeting you receive a personal invitation which also indicates that there will be other opportunities to discuss the appraisal results on a one-to-one basis. It makes it clear that everyone's contribution to the quality action phase will be vitally important.

IDENTIFYING REASONS FOR DIFFERENCES BETWEEN MEASUREMENTS AND STANDARDS   67

You are a most unusual person if you prefer Scenario A.

Change is unlikely to take place unless the results of quality appraisal are perceived as well-intentioned and constructive feedback. Communication should be:

- clear and to the point – however skilful the quality assurance group have been in involving colleagues, appraisal of standards and proposals for change can provoke anxiety – and anxiety feeds on uncertainty;
- specific – it is easier to understand 'in three cases telephones were not available on the same floor as residents' rooms' than to understand 'access standards were sometimes not met';
- as positive as possible – feedback should begin with good points from the appraisal, and personal criticism and blaming of individuals should be avoided;
- confidential – if specific individuals or groups are identified as contributing to poor quality, special steps should be taken to restrict the information to an appropriate sub-group;

- forward-looking – feedback should emphasize the opportunities for improvement and achievement of high quality which have been identified, rather than shame or blame associated with poor quality.
- corporate – feedback should emphasize that everyone in the agency is responsible for quality, be it good or poor, and that everyone will now be committed to helping to take action to meet the standard.

Before discussing quality action, it is important to try to identify reasons for the observed poor quality. It is worth asking questions similar to those which were asked about above-standard quality.

- Has measured performance fallen short of the standard on previous appraisal occasions? Why?
- Is the measured performance worse than on previous appraisal occasions? Why?
- Have there been significant changes in resources (including staff resources) since the last appraisal?
- Have there been changes in characteristics of service users since the last appraisal?
- Have similar deteriorations taken place in other similar service units?

Answering these and similar questions may be beyond the capability of your quality assurance group in its present form.

ACTIVITY 6.4

Consider the following quality initiatives.

- A group of colleagues working in a dementia day-care centre set up by a voluntary agency is carrying out a quality initiative to do with keeping daily activity diaries for each of the centre's users.

- A consortium of private residential home owners is working with a local social services department. A quality team has been set up to improve communication systems within a 'mixed economy' managed care scheme.

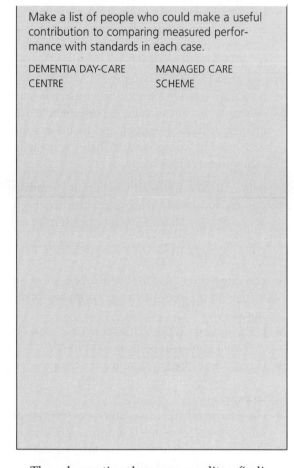

Make a list of people who could make a useful contribution to comparing measured performance with standards in each case.

DEMENTIA DAY-CARE   MANAGED CARE
CENTRE   SCHEME

The dementia day-care quality findings could quite probably be interpreted and appropriate action taken without involving anyone beyond the centre team. Quality in the managed care scheme is a more complex matter. It may be necessary to consult with colleagues from different professions, different management levels and different geographical areas.

No matter how much consultation takes place, it may not be possible to pin down all of the causes of poor quality. It is important to realize that causes are less important than ways of improving matters. Causes are only useful if they lead to ideas for action for improvement.

Your quality assurance group has a list of the most plausible reasons for the quality gap, and is now ready to identify action plans.

6.2 Identifying possible action plans

OBJECTIVES

By the end of this section you will be able to:

● comment on quality assurance group membership at this stage in quality assurance;

● describe a method for stimulating creative discussion of possible action plans.

In principle, there is an infinite number of ways of improving quality. At this stage in the quality cycle the group's task is the generation of a range of options. These must be:

● realistic;
● acceptable to people who will be affected by agreed changes;
● acceptable to managers and policy-makers responsible for resources;
● acceptable to managers and policy-makers ultimately accountable for the quality of service.

These conditions influence the membership of the quality assurance group. It may be important to have:

● representatives of the people who will be affected by the agreed changes (this could include users or carers or their representatives, as well as colleagues);
● management or others with some authority to approve or ease the implementation of action plans.

This revised group is referred to as the *action group*.

The action group must be as creative as possible in generating potential plans for action. One method for encouraging group creativity is known as brainstorming.

BRAINSTORMING

Brainstorming is a group activity which has been used to produce ideas in business, research and other settings since the 1950s.

One group member becomes the session leader. This could be the chair of the quality assurance group, or someone who has had previous experience of leading brainstorming groups. The session leader has a very important task. He or she must:

- encourage everyone to participate;
- collect as many ideas as possible by going repeatedly around the group;
- ask each person in turn to contribute an idea (a person may 'pass');
- allow no comments (positive or negative) about ideas while they are being contributed;
- record the group's ideas on a flipchart so that everyone can see them;
- when everyone 'passes' help the group to categorize the ideas generated.

Team members:

- contribute as many ideas as possible (no matter how 'extreme' or 'silly');
- make no comment on other people's contributions;
- build upon other people's contributions.

The leader then helps the group to categorize ideas, and possibly to begin to consider their feasibility.

By the end of this stage the group has a list of possible action plans and is ready to choose a suitable one.

6.3 Choosing the best action plan(s)

OBJECTIVES

By the end of this section you will be able to:

- list the points that quality action groups should consider in choosing an action plan;
- comment on the importance of consultation in choosing an action plan;
- comment on the relationships between quality and cost.

At this stage of the quality assurance cycle the quality action group has identified a number of possible plans. It must now choose the best one. But what does 'best' mean here?

The best action plan is the one which is most likely to bring about the greatest improvement in overall quality of service.

ACTIVITY 6.5

Think of a possible plan for improving quality in your own workplace. Now list the advantages and disadvantages it might have.

ADVANTAGES   DISADVANTAGES

Looking back at your lists of advantages and disadvantages, you can probably suggest some issues a quality action group might bear in mind when choosing their best plan.

The action plan must be likely to bring about the desired improvement in quality.

- How much improvement in quality will the plan bring about?
- Will it improve quality with reasonable effort?
- Will it improve quality within a reasonable time?
- Will its anticipated results be measurable the next time standards are appraised?

The action plan must be likely to be implemented.

- Who and what is likely to be affected by its implementation?
- Is it within existing policy and guidelines?
- Is it acceptable to senior management?
- Is it acceptable to colleagues?
- Are suitable, enthusiastic colleagues available to 'champion' it?

Finally, the action plan must be financially realistic.

- Will the plan save money?
- Can it be implemented within current or easily obtainable resources?
- Will it cost a lot to implement compared with what it will achieve?

Answering these questions is not easy. The action group may not be able to answer them without a further round of consultation and discussion. Wide consultation has two benefits. It may produce new ideas, and it also keeps colleagues informed about likely changes.

Discussion of the resource implications of the proposed plan is likely to be lively.

Donabedian (1986) put forward three points he thought the US government should consider when trying to improve the quality of health care.

- Quality costs money.
- Money does not necessarily buy quality.
- Some improvements in quality are not worth the added cost.

The costs of making improvements and of continuing with 'poor' quality should both be set out. The impact of the planned quality improvement on resources for other aspects of

Quality is our sole concern – within the 10% efficiency savings of course – we are totally committed to quality of service

ACTIVITY 6.6

Look back at the discussion of quality and cost in Section 3.4.

What resource points could a quality action group make in trying to persuade senior management of the benefits of their plans?

service should also be borne in mind. Robbing Peter to pay Paul is not good quality action.

Once selected, the action plan should be set out in detail. It should specify:

- the steps involved;
- the time it will take to carry out each step;
- the people responsible for each step;
- dates for progress reports;
- dates for publicity initiatives;
- a final completion date;
- a date for reappraisal of the standard;
- a date for review of the standard.

Upon completion of this stage, the action group has chosen a 'best' plan for quality action. The next stage is to implement it.

6.4 Implementing the action plan(s)

OBJECTIVES

By the end of this section you will be able to:

- outline some general principles of managing change;
- describe the role of a quality 'project manager';
- comment on the importance of communication in bringing about change.

In the last stage the action group selected an action plan. One of its features was that it was 'likely to be implemented'. In this stage the group is about to find out how good their judgement was about that. They have consulted widely and have obtained a degree of agreement from managers, colleagues and other people likely to be affected by the proposed plan. That agreement will now be put to the test.

Social care is complex. Care delivered to any one group of clients may be the end result of many different activities carried out in many different organizations.

ACTIVITY 6.7

Look back at the box you completed in Section 2.3 (p. 12), where you made a list of all the people who could influence the quality of care for a client in your own workplace.

- Now rate each of these people (or groups) according to how easy it would be to change their contribution to your client's care. (Rate them on a scale of 1 to 5, where 5 means they would be very easy to change and 1 means it would be almost impossible.)

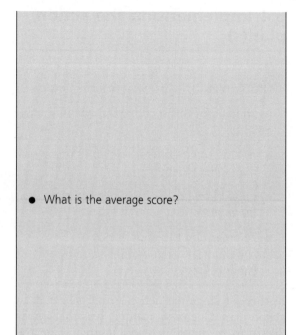

● What is the average score?

In a complex area like social care, changing the routine activities of one person can have an impact, however small, on all of the others. You will remember that we noted in Section 2.3 that 'quality is everyone's business'. In this section we rephrase that as follows:

'Quality improvement is everyone's willingness to change what they do for the sake of the improvement'.

Change in any organization can be difficult to bring about. However carefully plans are thought through, the implementation phase can cause disruption and stress. This is particularly so if the organization concerned has gone through difficult changes in the past.

ACTIVITY 6.8

● Make a list of anxieties that colleagues in your own workplace might have if 'quality improvements' were proposed.

Did you include these?

● The proposals are just disguised financial cuts.
● The proposals will mean more work.
● The proposals will mean loss of status.
● The proposals will mean working with people who don't know what they are doing.
● We won't know how to handle the new tasks.
● There won't be any training.
● There will be more pointless paperwork.
● The proposals aren't what clients really need.

You may also have realized that the emphasis in previous sections of this book on consultation and careful communication when planning changes is designed to defuse some of these anxieties. Without good communication and maximum involvement of colleagues in planning change, its implementation is likely to be superficial at best.

At the implementation stage, too, everyone affected by the change must be:

● given regular information updates;
● encouraged to put forward their points of view;
● listened to;
● allowed to challenge ideas.

This approach has another important advantage. Feedback from a wider range of colleagues or clients could reveal a flaw in the plan that has not been taken into account. This could mean revising the plan.

Consultation and communication are vital – but implementing the action plan needs more. When it comes to actually getting something done, it can be helpful to identify one individual who is responsible for making sure that progress takes place. That person is the quality *project manager*.

ACTIVITY 6.9

Think of someone in your own workplace who would make a good quality project manager.

Make a list of the reasons you chose that person.

Does your project manager have the following?

- Knowledge appropriate to the action to be taken.
- Skills appropriate to the action to be taken.
- Experience in the area where change is to take place.
- Professional credibility with colleagues in the area where change is to take place.
- Ability to persuade and motivate people.
- Ability to smooth out conflict.
- A good network of contacts with colleagues, managers and other relevant groups.
- Good time management skills.
- An organized approach to paperwork.

At the end of Section 6.3 we described a plan for quality action. It included -

- the steps involved;
- the time it will take to carry out each step;

And I thought the lift would be a great improvement

- the people responsible for each step;
- dates for progress reports;
- dates for publicity initiatives;
- a final completion date;
- a date for reappraisal of the standard;
- a date for review of the standard.

The quality project manager is responsible for the progress of the plan. If major changes are intended, this could include:

- organizing action group meetings;
- organizing *ad hoc* working group meetings;
- organizing meetings with colleagues, managers and other relevant people;
- preparing and circulating minutes from meetings to relevant people;
- making personal contact with people likely to be affected by the action plan;
- monitoring of deadlines;
- issuing periodic reminders;
- smoothing out disputes;
- providing progress reports;
- making sure communication is flowing smoothly;
- informal networking, talking and listening;
- producing a quality action newsletter or contributing to a more general one;
- organizing a quality action noticeboard in a prominent place;
- keeping a record of all correspondence and documentation relevant to the action plan.

Fortunately, many quality action plans involve only a few people, and the project manager's task need not be quite so complex!

6.5 Reappraising the standard

OBJECTIVES

By the end of this section you will be able to:

- identify possible outcomes of quality action;
- comment on reappraisal scheduling.

Reappraisal of a standard means re-examining performance using the same indicators and measurement techniques as in the original appraisal. Once the action plan has been fully completed, reappraisal should confirm the beneficial effects of the action taken. However, some caution should be exercised. Change can take time, and reappraising a standard too soon after implementing action can have discouraging (and basically inaccurate) results.

If the standard is still not being met, then further quality action is required. The quality assurance group must consider whether the standard is unrealistic, or whether circumstances changed during the period of their quality activities. If the standard is appropriate and the circumstances are much the same, another action plan is required. Valuable lessons may, however, have been learned from trying to implement the first one.

If the standard is now being met, further reappraisal should take place as scheduled. Reappraisal schedules are an important aspect of overall quality management.

Reappraisal is the last stage of the quality cycle. We have now discussed all the stages of quality appraisal and quality action.

One further task remains. This is the review of standards.

6.6 Reviewing standards

OBJECTIVES

By the end of this section you will be able to:

- identify reasons for reviewing standards.

From time to time (possibly once per year) the quality assurance group should review the standards they have set and agreed upon. They should discuss the results of quality appraisals and reappraisals and determine any action required.

Difficulties may have emerged in measurement or other aspects of the appraisal of a particular standard. The group could decide to rewrite the standard to be more explicit, or to choose new indicators or measurement techniques. For another standard, records might show that the standard has been consistently exceeded. Here the group could try to improve quality by writing more demanding requirements into the standard. Alternatively, the group might decide that it is time to develop a new standard or even to consider a new topic – that is, to repeat the cycle.

In these sections you have considered approaches to quality action. You have now completed the second half of the quality cycle.

Self-Assessment Exercises

Now that you have completed Chapter 6 you may find it helpful to check your progress by trying these self-assessment exercises. You will find our suggested answers at the end of the book.

Exercise 13

Complete the following sentences by choosing a word or phrase from those listed.

1. Higher standards should be set if _____ _____.

    quality consistently meets standards
    poor quality has been identified
    average quality has been identified
    consistent quality has been identified

2. Where sub-standard quality has been identi-fied, quality action groups should always _____.

    publicize their findings immediately
    lower their standards
    try to provide feedback in a constructive and diplomatic way
    make sure that the people involved in that service area are the last to know

3. A quality action group may need additional members if _____.

    quality is consistently high
    interpreting results requires new perspec-tives
    quality is consistently low
    standards are inappropriate

4. In brainstorming _____ _____.

    ideas are not discussed until everyone has contributed fully
    some group members are allowed to stay silent
    the group leader stays silent
    people must be careful not to put 'silly' ideas forward

5. According to Donabedian, some improve-ments in quality are not worth _____.
    encouraging
    careful measurement

the added cost
the outcome

6. Standards should be reviewed _____ _____.

    if quality is still poor
    when the quality assurance group has completed other tasks
    if circumstances change
    on a regular scheduled basis

Exercise 14

Which of the following statements are true? Write true or false in the space provided.

1. If quality is consistently high there is no point in trying to improve it. _____

2. Feedback on the results of quality appraisal should be specific. _____

3. Quality action can never be taken by a small group. _____

4. Quality action plans should be financially realistic. _____

5. Quality action groups should have clear strategies for consultation and communica-tion. _____

6. Standards can be reappraised too soon. _____

Exercise 15

1. Give two reasons why quality might improve between successive quality   appraisals.

2. Give two reasons why a quality action plan might not succeed in improving quality.

3. Give two reasons for selecting someone as project manager for the implementation of quality action.

Exercise 16

1. Outline the stages of quality action.

2. Identify four anxieties that colleagues might have about proposed quality action.

3. Suggest two things a quality action group might do if an action plan has been imple-mented and quality has still not improved.

Quality assured in social care

Introduction to quality assured in social care

OBJECTIVES

By the end of Chapter Seven you will be able to:

● place the two case studies presented in Part Three in their geographical and professional contexts;

● state personal learning objectives for Part Three.

Part Three contains two case studies. Each of them describes a quality initiative undertaken in a different social care setting. The first took place in a Supported Housing development for frail and vulnerable older people, set up by a Health and Social Services Community Trust in partnership with a Housing Association. The second was undertaken by a Community Stroke Rehabilitation Team within a Health and Social Services Community Trust.

Each case study is from a Northern Ireland setting. Local authorities in Northern Ireland do not have responsibility for Social Services. There are therefore no Social Services Departments as such. Social services in Northern Ireland are commissioned through four Health and Social Services Boards, which also have responsibility for commissioning both hospital and community health care. Each of the quality initiatives described in Part Three was undertaken within the Eastern Health and Social Services Board (EHSSB) area. The EHSSB is responsible for health and social care in the greater Belfast area and in parts of Counties Antrim and Down. Social care is provided in Northern Ireland by a mix of statutory, voluntary and private sector agencies. Statutory services are provided by Health and Social Services Trusts, within which there are a variety of arrangements for professional involvement in the management of Social Services. Each of these Trusts has a Director of Social Services who is a member of the Trust Executive.

The main difference is that Social Services in

ACTIVITY 7.1

List ways in which the organization of Social Services in Northern Ireland is the *same* as that in England and Wales (or Scotland), and ways in which it is *different*.

SAME   DIFFERENT

Northern Ireland are organized as part of an integrated system of health and personal social services. The 'internal market' of commissioning and provision and the 'mixed economy' of statutory, voluntary and private provision are very similar. Several recent government statements have suggested that closer links between social services and health care are likely to be encouraged elsewhere in the UK.

One potential advantage of the Northern Irish system is that it is easier to set up interprofessional care teams. The two quality initiatives described in the next chapters are interprofessional.

ACTIVITY 7.2

One of the initiatives you are about to read aimed to improve the quality of care provided for recovering stroke patients. Imagine you are a social care professional involved in a quality initiative in that setting. Make a note of the particular contribution you would expect your *health care* colleagues to make.

You would probably expect them to comment on the aspects of the service for which they were directly responsible. Physiotherapists might comment on facilities for improving mobility, occupational therapists might comment on household adaptations, and GPs might want to comment on hospital/community liaison. You may also have noted that health care colleagues might have a broad perspective on approaches and techniques in quality assurance, based on their experience of quality assurance and audit in health care.

ACTIVITY 7.3

Look back to Section 2.3, 'Who Sets Quality Standards?', for some information on quality assurance in health care.

Each of the chapters of this book you have worked through so far has set specific learning objectives for you. It is more difficult to do this for the next two chapters. What you learn from each of the case studies will depend on your personal experience of similar settings and on what you have learned from the earlier parts of this book. We have set more general objectives.

OBJECTIVES

By the end of Part Three you should be able to:

- compare the different approaches to quality appraisal and improvement adopted in each of the case studies and in earlier examples in this book;

- compare and comment on quality teams in each of the case studies, and relate them to earlier sections of this book;

- compare and comment on the likely impact of each initiative on the overall quality of service delivered;

- make suggestions for the further development of quality initiatives in each of the settings described.

Your personal objectives should be more specific.

As you will see, the next two chapters depart from our usual workbook format. They are more straightforward descriptions of the quality initiatives. You will find it helpful to keep note of what you have learned as you go along, and to check back to your objectives at the end of each chapter.

ACTIVITY 7.4

Make a list of your own objectives for the next two chapters. You might like to look quickly back over earlier units to identify any areas you would like to clarify by learning about real examples of quality appraisal and improvement.

PERSONAL OBJECTIVES

Our exploration of each of the three quality initiatives follows the same outline. In each case we shall explore the following:

- background;
- aims;
- approach;
- standards;
- quality appraisal;
- quality action;
- impact
- plans for the future.

8 A case study from care of older people – the 'Fairholme' initiative

8.1 Background

The setting for this quality initiative is the Fairholme Supported Housing development. Fairholme was opened in December 1994 and is run jointly by Belfast Improved Housing and the South and East Belfast Health and Social Services Trust. Belfast Improved Housing is one of Northern Ireland's leading Housing Associations, and provides homes for families, single people and people with special needs throughout the greater Belfast area. South and East Belfast has an established reputation for successful innovation in domiciliary care management.

Fairholme is a unique scheme designed to cater for the needs of frail and vulnerable older people in an environment where they can achieve maximum levels of independence, privacy and dignity. There are 40 flatlets, with each tenant having secure tenancy and their own front door. Some have installed their own telephones, and most have their own television sets. In addition, tenants have access to central facilities, including a dining room providing a full meals service, and small kitchens and dining areas where snack meals can be prepared.

All Fairholme tenants have been assessed by the Trust's care managers as needing high levels of support. They often have complex needs relating to dementia, a history of mental illness, or problems associated with isolation, extreme fear of living alone or vulnerability to abuse. Each tenant has a written and agreed care plan and receives the necessary skilled care on a 24-hour basis. Tenants pay a full commercial charge

for hotel services and rent (£109.93 per week at the time of writing) and receive care free. Belfast Improved Housing provide and maintain the accommodation and the South and East Belfast Trust provides care services, catering, cleaning and personal laundry services through their core contract with the Eastern Health and Social Services Board. The Fairholme care team is led by a care manager (with a nursing background). There are 4 senior care assistants, 12 care assistants and a range of support staff.

There were several reasons for deciding to undertake the quality initiative. First, since Fairholme's older people are tenants rather than residents, Fairholme is not subject to the usual Inspection Unit monitoring. Both Belfast Improved Housing and the Trust felt that some substitute quality assurance procedure was very necessary. Secondly, there was an established quality culture in the Trust, in part as a result of quality requirements in health care contracts, and in part as a result of senior managers' foresight and commitment. Finally, and perhaps most importantly, the proposed quality initiative was thought to be a useful mechanism for winning staff over to the new ideas which underpinned Fairholme's establishment and operation.

Fairholme's opening coincided with the closure of a Residential Home, and several residents and staff chose to move into Fairholme. The majority of the Fairholme staff came from that home or from other residential settings. There was thus some danger that care practice at Fairholme would retain the institutional features of residential care. Involving tenants and staff in establishing Fairholme care standards would help to protect its special character.

8.2 Aims

The Fairholme initiative has three main aims.

- to assure and improve the quality of care provided to Fairholme tenants in line with the core values and aims of the Fairholme project itself;
- to provide objective evidence of Fairholme care quality which will be of use in accounting for both the Trust's and the Housing Association's investment in it;
- to involve and motivate both staff and tenants.

8.3 Approach

The overall approach adopted by the Fairholme team was concurrent records-based audit. The audit was based on standards set through consultation involving both staff and tenants.

Considerable time was devoted to identifying appropriate topics for standard setting, and to ensuring that all staff and all residents were fully involved in the process. Initially, senior staff meetings took place at which differences between the more conventional values of residential care and those of the Fairholme project were explored. There was particular emphasis on the implications of these differences for day-to-day practice. Broader staff meetings also took place in which existing good practice was documented along with potential areas for improvement. The general idea of quality assurance and standard setting was then discussed fully at tenants' meetings (which already took place regularly), and tenants were invited to identify improvement areas. The 25 per cent of tenants who had not attended the relevant meetings were asked to complete brief questionnaires.

A range of opportunities for improvement were identified from which broad areas for standard setting were developed. There were six key areas:

- decision-making;
- health care;
- physical environment;
- care practices;
- risk-taking;
- relatives and friends.

8.4 Standards

Standard setting was carried out through meetings of staff groups and of a specially set up tenants' group. The eventually agreed standards in each area were as follows.

Decision-making

All tenants living at Fairholme will be enabled, to the full extent of their abilities, to make their own decisions about all aspects of their lives.

Health care

All tenants will be facilitated in accessing health care services.

Physical environment

Fairholme will provide a safe environment, whereby tenants can retain an independent lifestyle.

Care practices

Staff practices in Fairholme will reflect an understanding of the core values which underpin promotion of quality care and good practice.

Risk-taking

All tenants will be enabled to maintain an independent lifestyle which may incur a degree of risk.

Relatives and friends

All relatives and friends will be encouraged to be involved and to participate in the care of tenants.

Once standards had been agreed, all staff were expected to be firmly committed to them and to acknowledge their personal responsibility for their implementation. Each tenant has a named key worker (who is a senior care assistant) and a named primary worker (who is a care assistant). They were to be responsible for implementation of the standards in the context of that individual tenant's care.

8.5 Quality appraisal

The first area to be tackled was decision-making. The standard which had been set was very broad, and there was extensive discussion of appropriate indicators. It was agreed that indicators had to be clear and easy to use. They also had to provide a fair assessment of the extent to which records provided evidence of tenants' involvement in decision-making. Each indicator was turned into a question and included in an Audit Form (see below).

It was also agreed that, since the total population of Fairholme tenants was only 40 people, audit of all case records could take place and sampling would therefore not be necessary.

Initial audit of care records was undertaken by a clerical assistant. A form was completed

---

Fairholme Audit Form No. 1

Standard   All tenants living at Fairholme are enabled, to the full extent of their abilities, to make their own decisions about all aspects of their lives

Audit date   18 September 1996
Audit target 100%

Indicator question   **Yes/No**

FA1
Are monthly tenants' meetings held?

FA2
Is tenant invited to attend?

FA3
Is tenant sent letters?

FA4
Does tenant attend meetings?

FA5
Is tenant involved in drawing up care plans?

FA6
Is tenant involved in changes made to care plans?

FA7
Are care plans written in user-
friendly language?

FA8
Is the tenant consulted about any decisions
made on his or her behalf?

FA9
Are relatives consulted about any decisions
made on the tenant's behalf?

FA10
Is there evidence of tenant involvement
in reviews?

for each tenant's record. Results were then pooled and entered in the second and third columns of the Summary Audit Report Form (see p. 85). The summary form and an accompanying report were then checked and validated by the care manager in consultation with senior colleagues.

8.6 Quality action

Audit results were discussed by staff and tenants and required action was agreed. The final column of the Audit Report Form was then completed as set out below.

8.7 Impact

The Fairholme audit had immediate practical consequences in changes in procedures for ensuring tenants' attendance at meetings, in improved record-keeping, and in renewed efforts to involve relatives in decision-making. Further discussion of the results from indicator 9 led to exploration of the family circumstances of tenants whose relatives had not been consulted. Some proved to have had limited contact with relatives, and staff agreed that special steps might be needed to support them.

As this was the first standard to be audited, staff also discussed the overall value of the exercise. The clerical assistant had had extra work to do, and other staff noted that they had paid more attention than usual to completion of records prior to the audit date. Despite that, it was generally agreed that it was good to see how close they had come to meeting the standard, and that the action needed for quality improvement seemed reasonable.

8.8 Plans for the future

The Fairholme team now intend to develop audit forms for the other five key areas. Once all audits have been completed, they will go back to the general discussion and survey method to see whether other areas for improvement can be identified. The care manager will make use of the audit data in preparing her annual report and in other activities designed to publicize the Fairholme approach to supporting frail older people.

8.9 Summary and discussion

The Fairholme quality initiative is clearly meeting its objectives (see Section 8.2). The quality of care has been improved, audit information has been used to demonstrate the effectiveness of the Fairholme approach, and both staff and tenants have found the exercise worthwhile. Fairholme has recently been awarded the UK National Charter Mark for public service quality.

Fairholme Summary Audit Report No. 1

Standard   All tenants living at Fairholme are enabled, to the full extent of their abilities, to make their own decisions about all aspects of their lives.

Audit date   18 September 1996

Total case notes   40
Audit target   100%
Achievement   56% to 100% (see below)

Indicator question	Yes/No	Percentage achievement	Comments/ action
FA1 Are monthly tenants' meetings held?	40 Yes	100	
FA2 Is tenant invited to attend?	40 Yes	100	
FA3 Is tenant sent letters?	40 Yes	100	Individual letters and agenda placed on noticeboard.
FA4 Does tenant attend meetings?	30 Yes 10 No	75	New strategy to be adopted of including agenda with letter and following up with individual discussion.
FA5 Is tenant involved in drawing up care plans?	40 Yes	100	
FA6 Is tenant involved in changes made to care plans?	35 Yes definitely 5 Yes probably	88	35 records showed clear evidence of involvement. In the other cases, records were unclear but staff knew that there had been involvement. Staff to improve record-keeping.
FA7 Are care plans written in user-friendly language?	40 Yes	100	
FA8 Is the tenant consulted about any decisions made on his or her behalf?	40 Yes	100	
FA9 Are relatives consulted about any decisions made on the tenant's behalf?	32 Yes 3 Yes (no signature) 6 No	80	Staff to discuss and determine reasons for negative cases.
FA10 Is there evidence of tenant involvement in reviews?	40 Yes	100	

A case study from community stroke rehabilitation – the 'hospital at home' initiative

9.1 Background

The setting for this quality initiative is a community rehabilitation scheme set up by the North Down and Ards Community Health and Social Services Trust. The Trust serves a population of approximately 140 000 living in a geographical area of some 460 square kilometres. The area includes a number of relatively affluent commuter towns and villages along the southern shore of Belfast Lough, and a larger but much less populous rural hinterland. At the time of collecting information for this case study, hospital services in the area were provided by a separate Hospitals Trust (with specialist services also provided by larger Hospital Trusts in Belfast). There has subsequently been a merger between the Community Trust and the local Hospitals Trust.

Northern Ireland has a high incidence of cerebrovascular disorders, and rehabilitation services provided in hospital day-care and out-patient settings are over-subscribed. There are also problems of access for patients living in rural areas. The aim of the Hospital at Home Community Stroke Rehabilitation Scheme is to provide a locally accessible domiciliary service which assists clients towards independence and supports families in their role as carers. There is systematic liaison with hospital consultants and other professionals and with GPs and local vol-untary organizations. Patients are discharged from hospital sooner than might otherwise be possible, and every effort is made to ensure that there is continuity between hospital and domi-ciliary rehabilitation. Referrals are accepted from GPs and from hospital physicians, and clients generally remain in the scheme for periods of between 8 and 12 weeks. The Com-munity Rehabilitation team includes a social worker, three community care workers, a phys-iotherapist, an occupational therapist, a speech and language therapist and a community nurse (who also acts as co-ordinator). All have received specialist training for work with clients who have had strokes. There is also part-time secretarial and clerical support.

During their time with the scheme all clients are assessed by each professional, and relevant treatment, equipment and support are then pro-vided. The social worker and community care workers have particular responsibilities for helping clients and their families to come to terms with the personal, emotional, financial and social effects of their stroke. Prior to dis-charge, clients are referred to appropriate com-munity services for continuing care.

The quality initiative was first proposed because of the novelty of the provision. It was hoped that it would not only assure and im-prove quality, but also provide evidence which would contribute to an overall evaluation which had been a condition of funding. It was also recognized that normal lines of professional monitoring and accountability might have been weakened by the multiprofessional nature of the scheme. A strong internal quality system therefore seemed important. Finally, team members were aware that stroke patients' progress is most rapid soon after they suffer their stroke. Clients' views of the success of the scheme might change once their progress had begun to slow down. A survey of patients' views subsequent to discharge from the scheme was therefore proposed as part of the quality initiative.

9.2 Aims

The Hospital at Home initiative has three main aims:

- to assure and improve the quality of care provided to clients;
- to provide objective evidence of the quality of service being provided;
- to acquire feedback from clients discharged from the scheme.

9.3 Approach

The overall approach adopted by the Hospital at Home team included standard setting and concurrent records audit within the DySSSy model (see Chapter 2 (p. 14)) and a satisfaction survey of discharged clients. The broad idea was discussed with senior managers in the Trust, but once initial approval was obtained the initiative was entirely designed and implemented by the local team. The initiative was set up relatively early in the life of the scheme, and initial team discussions revealed understandable concern about co-ordination of assessments and treatment visits.

9.4 Standards

Four standards were written and relevant process and outcome criteria worked out. The standards were as follows.

Standard One

Every client referred is assessed within 1 week of referral.

Standard Two

Individual team members carry out a relevant assessment in partnership with the client and his or her carer(s) and agree a plan of action within 1 week of referral.

Standard Three

Every client has his or her progress reassessed 3 months after discharge.

Standard Four

Team members take client choice into account when arranging visits.

9.5 Quality appraisal

Records were scrutinized for 33 per cent of clients. Every third record was picked out from an alphabetical listing so as obtain a random sample. The results of the scrutiny were as set out below.

Standard One

Every client referred is assessed within 1 week of referral.
87 per cent compliance.

Standard Two

Individual team members carry out a relevant assessment in partnership with the client and his or her carer(s) and agree a plan of action within 1 week of referral.
75 per cent compliance (there was some difficulty with this standard, as immediate difficulties tended to be dealt with outside the assessment process, and sometimes without consultation with client and carers).

Standard Three

Every client has his or her progress reassessed 3 months after discharge.
100 per cent compliance.

Standard Four

Team members take client choice into account when arranging visits.
100 per cent compliance.

The patient satisfaction survey was carried out using a short and simple questionnaire which allowed clients and their carers to identify good and not so good aspects of the care they had received, and to make suggestions for improvement. It was administered to 25 of the 47 clients who had been discharged from the scheme at that time. Administration took place along with the reassessment which took place 3 months after discharge.

The survey revealed broad satisfaction with the scheme and identified two opportunities for improvement. A newsletter was suggested as a way to maintain links with the scheme, and it was pointed out that staff participation in clients' and carers' group meetings could be better.

9.6 Quality Action

Standard One

Every client referred is assessed within 1 week of referral.
Although compliance with this standard was high, it was noted in discussion of results that the standard should have included reference to satisfactory issue of equipment. It is now being rewritten.

Standard Two

Individual team members carry out a relevant assessment in partnership with the client and his or her carer(s) and agree a plan of action within 1 week of referral.
This standard is being rewritten to take account of action taken prior to assessments.

Standard Three

Every client has his or her progress reassessed 3 months after discharge.
No action.

Standard Four

Team members take client choice into account when arranging visits.
No action.

Action has also been taken in response to the questionnaire results. Each team member has been asked to make a brief presentation to the clients' and carers' group, and all have been encouraged to attend more often. A newsletter has been produced which has been very well received.

9.7 Impact

The Hospital at Home quality initiative has helped staff to identify aspects of their assessment procedures where quality could be improved. Prior to appraising standards they were less aware of the significance of equipment issue and of immediate response to difficulty in the quality of their service. The exercise also provided evidence of overall satisfaction with the service, and helped staff to feel that their innovation was worthwhile. This evidence will be used in reports to the Trust and to senior professional managers. There have also been practical improvements to quality. Links with discharged patients have been improved, and the newsletter helps both old and new clients to feel supported by each other and by staff.

9.8 Plans for the future

Audit is to be repeated on an annual basis, and standards are being developed for other aspects of the service.

9.9 Summary and discussion

The Hospital at Home quality initiative has achieved its objectives. There have been quality improvements, objective evidence has been provided, and feedback has been obtained from discharged clients.

ACTIVITY 9.1

Look back to the objectives you set for Part Three. If you have achieved them, you should now be able to:

- compare the different approaches to quality appraisal and improvement adopted in each of the case studies and in earlier examples in this book;

- compare and comment on quality teams in each of the case studies, and relate them to earlier sections of this book;

- compare and comment on the likely impact of each initiative on the overall quality of service delivered;

- make suggestions for the further development of quality initiatives in each of the settings described.

Check to see if you have achieved these objectives.

You also set personal objectives.

Check to see if you have achieved your own objectives.

PART FOUR

More quality assured

Developing quality assurance in social care

OBJECTIVES

By the end of Chapter Ten you will be able to:

- comment on likely future developments in quality assurance in social care;

- estimate the extent to which this book has helped you to learn about quality assurance in social care;

- make personal plans for further involvement in quality assurance in social care.

10.1 How important is quality assurance likely to become in social care?

Many of the ideas and techniques you have learned about in this book had their origins in manufacturing industry or in health care. They are steadily becoming very important in service industries and in other public sector areas, such as education.

You may have included arguments based on clients' expectations of high quality, or on their basic right to the best possible service. You may also have suggested that cost-effective quality assurance can actually save money. As a professional you may have added that it is important that people closely involved in social care carry out their own quality assurance because, if they do not, there is a strong likelihood that someone else will! Several recent government statements have hinted that legislation requiring social care audit is being planned. It is likely that these requirements will be similar to the ones included in the 1990 NHS reforms and developed further in the 'New NHS' 1997 white paper. Finally, if you are working in a market set-

ACTIVITY 10.1

Look back to Section 3.2 (p. 18), where we considered reasons for developing quality assurance procedures in social care settings.

Now that you have almost finished this book, use the ideas from Section 3.2 and the expertise you now have to make a list of arguments you could put to your senior managers for establishing some form of quality assurance in your own area of work.

ting, you may have pointed out that gaining a quality kitemark would enhance the reputation of your agency and help you to win contracts.

10.2 What have you learned from this workbook?

ACTIVITY 10.2

Look back to the aims we set out for you and to the personal objectives you wrote for yourself in 'About this Workbook' (p. viii).

Check whether they have been achieved. You should now:

● understand what quality assurance is;

● know something of the origins of quality assurance;

● appreciate the importance of quality assurance for social care;

● be able to describe a number of quality assurance techniques;

● be able to evaluate the potential of these techniques for your own workplace;

● want to know more about quality assurance;

● be keen to become more involved in quality assurance;

More importantly, we hope you have also achieved your personal objectives.

10.3 How can you go on to be more involved in quality assurance?

You have now reached the end of this workbook, but we hope it is only the beginning of your involvement in quality assurance. We hope that you will use the list of 'Useful Reading' which follows to find out more. We also hope that you will go on to become practically involved in quality assurance. You may be able to join existing quality groups or to contact some of the organizations we mention in Section 3.5 (p. 27). Alternatively, you may want to generate local initiatives in your own workplace. Whatever you decide to do, we wish you every success in your pursuit of the highest quality social care.

Solutions to self-assessment exercises

Chapter 2 (p.15)

Exercise 1

1. fit for purpose
2. who is defining it
3. standards
4. the resources devoted to care
5. easier to measure
6. has an interest in the quality of the product or service

Exercise 2

1. False

Definitions of quality can often include some reference to 'reasonable' cost or 'value for money'. However, quality does not necessarily imply expensive – look back at the examples we gave about cars.

2. False

Quality can be poor or mediocre, as well as excellent.

3. True

Standards can be more or less specific and can permit objective measurement or only subjective judgement, but they always state what has to be achieved.

4. False

The process of care includes face-to-face interaction, but it also includes things like record keeping and care-planning which need not involve face-to-face interaction.

5. False

In some settings subjective judgement may be all that is possible.

6. True

Professional bodies award the license to practise to people who have demonstrated that their practice meets minimum standards of competence.

Exercise 3

There are no completely right answers to this exercise, but check your answers with these suggestions.

1a. Standards might be difficult to set in social care because much of social care is interpersonal and involves things which are difficult to measure, like empathy and understanding.
1b. Social care takes place in a complex organizational setting in which professionals, managers and clients might all have different ideas about appropriate standards.

2a. If one person is responsible for quality, everyone else may decide it is not their business.
2b. The more people that are involved, the more ideas and information will be available.

3a. Clients are the final customers and are well placed to make judgements on the overall outcomes of care delivered, whether it meets needs and how it could be improved.
3b. Clients have a basic right to be involved in decisions about their own care, and this includes decisions about standards.

Exercise 4

Again there are no absolutely right answers, but check your definitions with the ones in the glossary. You might also like to check your definition of quality with the one you wrote when completing Chapter 1. Has it changed?

Chapter 3 (p.29)

Exercise 5

1. up to standard
2. they have power to commit resources to it
3. all of these
4. at least as long ago as ancient Egyptian times
5. quality assurance
6. cost less than the costs of poor quality they prevent

Exercise 6

1. False

Quality is only completely assured once both halves of the quality cycle have been completed. This means both quality appraisal and quality action must have taken place.

2. True

Quality assurance activities benefit greatly from systematic and supportive management. Integration with other management tasks such as planning, policy-making and resource allocation can also be helpful.

3. False

Even if standards have been fully met and quality is high, there may still be opportunities for improvement, and thus a need for quality action.

4. True

You may however have noted the existence of the Inspection Units and of several government statements encouraging quality assurance in social care.

5. True

In areas where there is a physical product (like catering services) or where there is a relatively straightforward administrative process (like maintaining admission records), techniques from manufacturing industry may be entirely appropriate.

6. True

Poor communication can lead to professionals not understanding clients' needs or knowing their histories, to clients' developing inaccurate or incomplete expectations of service, to poor interprofessional liaison, and to many other failures of both process and outcome.

Exercise 7

There are no completely right answers to this exercise, but check your answers with these suggestions.

1a. Good communication ensures that everyone involved knows what they have to do.
1b. People can feel threatened when quality assurance procedures are set up for the first time. Good communication can help to defuse these anxieties.

2a. After the Industrial Revolution workers were much less likely to know their customers personally. That meant that they did not know their requirements in detail.
2b. After the Industrial Revolution many workers worked on assembly lines and were only responsible for parts of products. They often had little commitment to the overall quality of the product.

3a. Poor social care quality may lead to client complaint and even litigation. Clients may have to be financially compensated or given further service.
3b. Clients who receive poor-quality social care may need further service later in life which would not have been necessary if they had received a higher quality service in the first instance.

Exercise 8

Again there are no absolutely right answers, but check your definitions with the ones in the glossary. You might also like to check your definition of quality assurance with the one you wrote when completing Chapter 1. Has it changed?

Chapter 5 (p.62)

Exercise 9

1. are good at summarizing other people's contributions
2. the easier it will be to write a standard for it
3. the level of performance required to satisfy the standard
4. can lead to too much attention being paid to records for their own sake
5. contain a mix of open and closed questions.
6. identify instances of poor quality for subsequent detailed investigation and review

Exercise 10

1. False

There are advantages and disadvantages to having volunteers only. They may be very motivated, but may not include people who have the necessary expertise or who may be significant in facilitating quality action.

2. True

Group facilitators make sure the practicalities of group arrangements are attended to, ensure that all members have a fair chance to contribute, encourage frank and open debate, summarize discussion during and after meetings and, when appropriate, suggest additional sources of information. Skilled facilitators can do this without appearing to dominate proceedings.

3. False

There are several reasons for selecting a first quality topic. It could be selected because of particularly poor quality, but it could also be selected because it is likely to produce an early and obvious quality improvement or because it is some time since the topic was considered. Selecting a first topic is a decision quality groups should come to after careful discussion and possibly consultation with colleagues from outside the group.

4. False

Retrospective audit examines case notes and records for clients who are no longer receiving service. Direct observation of service is thus not possible.

5. False

Focus group procedures are designed to let group members talk about a broad topic in their own way and from their own perspective. Moderators usually have a list of sub-topics they hope the group will discuss, but they deliberately lead the group gently and intervene as little as possible.

6. True

Samples should be chosen to represent the population from which they are selected as closely as possible. For example, if the group of clients whose care is being appraised is 90 per cent female, the sample selected for interview should not be 90 per cent male.

Exercise 11

There are no completely right answers to this exercise, but check your answers with these suggestions.

1a. Effective groups are likely to have clear and agreed ideas about the purpose of the group.
1b. Effective groups are likely to agree about who does what in the group.

2a. Indicators which are very general and lack specificity are difficult to measure. This could lead to disagreement about the extent to which the standard has been achieved and about the action necessary for improvement.
2b. Some indicators are very specific but are not very clearly related to the standard which is being appraised. This, too, could lead to disagreement about how to interpret observations.

3a. Postal questionnaires are useful if relatively large numbers of responses are required and if there are resources for follow-up mailings.
3b. Postal questionnaires are useful if the questions to be asked are mostly closed

questions or questions which, although open, can be answered fairly briefly.

Exercise 12

Again there are no absolutely right answers but check your answers, with these suggestions.

1. The stages should include establishing the quality group, identifying a topic and if necessary sub-topics, writing the standard(s), agreeing indicators, selecting and piloting observation procedures and measuring instruments, making observations and measurements, and comparing measurements with standards.
2. SMART indicators (see p. 46) were Specific, Measurable, Achievable, Relevant and Targeted. Perhaps you can think of other features which would be important in your workplace.
3. Interviewers can help interviewees who have problems with written material. They can also encourage interviewees to explore attitudes and feelings in depth. On the other hand, interviewers may unconsciously influence respondents. They are also expensive to employ.

Chapter 6 (p.76)

Exercise 13

1. quality consistently meets standards
2. try to provide feedback in a constructive and diplomatic way
3. interpreting results requires new perspectives
4. ideas are not discussed until everyone has contributed fully
5. the added cost
6. on a regular scheduled basis

Exercise 14

1. False

There is always room for improvement. It is a basic principle of quality assurance that quality groups should work just as hard at improving good quality as they do at rectifying poor quality.

2. True

Specific feedback is more likely to lead to effective quality action because it will be easier for colleagues to know what they are expected to improve. Negative feedback which is not specific can be demoralizing, as the person who receives it can feel powerless to do anything about it. They may even think it applies to all aspects of their work.

3. False

If the quality standard which has been appraised applies to work done by a small group of people in a relatively isolated organizational setting, it may be quite possible for action only to involve the same small number of people. In theory, one person could carry out a quality initiative on their own work and involve no-one else.

4. True

If necessary resources cannot be obtained the quality action plan will be unsuccessful. Unrealistic plans can also lead to conflict and resentment when it has to be made clear that resources are not available. Making sure that initiatives have the support and involvement of senior managers from the beginning can help to prevent this kind of situation from occurring.

5. True

Quality action often involves change, and change provokes anxiety. Clear communication and wide consultation can help to defuse anxiety.

6. True

Time should be allowed for the full acceptance and implementation of the action plan before the standard is reappraised.

Exercise 15

There are no completely right answers to this exercise, but check your answers with these suggestions.

1a. An action plan has been successful.
1b. There has been some change in external cir-

cumstances, e.g. in resources available, staff involved or clients concerned.

2a. It has not had the support of professionals, managers or clients concerned.

2b. It has not been properly followed up and managed.

3a. They have technical and interpersonal skills appropriate to the action to be taken.

3b. They have good networks and high credibility in the areas where action is to be taken.

Exercise 16

Again there are no absolutely right answers, but check your answers against these suggestions.

1. The stages should include interpreting the results of appraisal, providing feedback, considering the membership of the quality group, identifying possible action plans, choosing the best plan, implementing the plan, reappraising the standard, and reviewing standards.

2. Colleagues might be worried that proposals might lead to more work, that there will be insufficient training, that the proposals will not meet client need, or that the proposals are cutbacks in disguise.

3. The group could look again at the two appraisals to see whether the results have been misinterpreted, or whether a different action plan might have been a better idea. Alternatively, they could review the standard to see if it was unrealistic.

Glossary of terms

Accreditation
The process by which an agency or organization evaluates and recognizes a programme of study or an institution as meeting predetermined standards.

Arm's-length inspection
System for monitoring care involving assessors who are external to the organization providing it.

Assurance
A statement or assertion intended to inspire confidence; a guarantee.

Audit
A methodical review or investigation; observation leading to a review or report.

Brainstorming
Group discussion technique designed to encourage production of a large number of ideas from which the best can be selected.

British Standards Institution
Organization responsible for setting UK national standards for a wide range of products and services; began with standards for engineering products, electrical goods and safety equipment, but now has a much wider remit; also responsible for BS5750, which sets standards for quality assurance systems and procedures.

Charter
Collection of standards statements committing an organization to specified levels of quality; can apply to products or services, but most frequently developed in public sector service contexts as in the Patients' Charter.

Client satisfaction
The extent to which care is regarded favourably by clients; often assessed by questionnaires or (less frequently) focus groups.

Code of conduct
Collection of rules for the regulation of professional behaviour, breach of which can result in disciplinary action, possibly including removal of the professional's licence to practise.

Competence
Knowledge, skills and personal attitudes necessary for the performance of professional tasks at acceptable levels of quality (see 'licence to practise' below).

Contract
A legal agreement committing two or more people or groups to do stipulated things; in social care an agreement between a purchaser and a provider of service in which the provider is committed to provision of service of specified quality in exchange for funding.

Cost-effective
Able to achieve intended objective(s) or meet standards with the minimum necessary use of resources.

Criterion
Specification of expected or desired quality of a product or service; often taken to be more specific than a standard and to permit measurement (see 'indicator' below). A number of criteria may be developed for one standard.

Effectiveness
The extent to which something achieves intended objective(s).

	The extent to which a product is fit for its purpose or care improves health, well-being and quality of life.
Efficiency	Producing maximum goods or delivering maximum service with minimum expenditure of resources.
Equity	Fairness, impartiality; in health and social care the fair distribution of resources for care, ensuring even-handedness and lack of discrimination in access to care.
Evaluation	A systematic process determining the extent to which a product is fit for its purpose or a service is successful in the achievement of predetermined objectives.
Feedback	Knowledge of results; information collected regarding the effectiveness of care; often particularly associated with measures of **client satisfaction**.
Indicator	Detailed and measurable specification of desired quality of a product or service associated with a more general standard statement. A number of indicators are usually developed for one standard.
International Standards Organization	World-wide standard-setting body. ISO9000 is the international equivalent of BS5750 (see 'British Standards Institute' above).
Inspection	Examining products after they have been produced so as to reject substandard ones. Substandard products can be either discarded or modified to meet standards.
	Scrutiny of facility or operation by external assessors (see 'arm's-length inspection' above).
Interpersonal care	Aspects of care involving interaction with clients.
Kitemark	An indication that quality has been evaluated by an external body and found to have met standards. Originally a stamp on goods tested for safety by the British Standards Institution.
Licence to practise	Legal document awarded by professional bodies to people who are able to demonstrate that they have reached specific levels of professional competence, usually following a period of recognized training, and that they are thus fit to practise. A public guarantee to potential clients that professionals have achieved specific levels of competence.
Monitoring	Observation and recording of events over time; implies comparison with standards.
Moral	Aspects of care requiring ethical judgement or reference to value systems.
Objective	Unbiased; factual; not influenced by the attitudes or opinions of an observer; easy for observers to agree upon.
Outcome	End results. In social care a change in the health, well-being or quality of life of a client that can be attributed to previous care.
Outcome quality	The extent to which standards set for the outcomes of care are met.

Process	An organized series of events or activities designed to achieve production of a product or delivery of a service. In social care all of the components of care, including needs assessment, allocation and targeting of resources, care planning, face-to-face involvement with clients, record-keeping, case review and after-care monitoring.
Process quality	The extent to which standards set for production processes or for the various components of care process are achieved.
Purchaser provider system	Market system in which purchasers (Health Authorities or Social Services Department) buy services they need for their population, paying providers (statutory, voluntary or independent agencies) for these services. Generally involves a legally binding contract between the two.
Quality	Degree or standard of excellence; a distinguishing characteristic or attribute; in health and social care includes such aspects as accessibility, relevance, effectiveness, equity, efficiency, economy and social acceptability.
Quality action	Activities designed to improve quality or to bring it up to a standard. Second half of the quality cycle. Plans and activities following the identification of a gap between standards set and quality achieved.
Quality action group	Team of people responsible for planning and facilitating action resulting from quality appraisal; may be identical with the quality assurance group or may have modified membership in the light of specific issues to be tackled.
Quality appraisal	A series of activities including standard setting, measurement and interpretation of measurements, designed to determine the extent to which a product is fit for its purpose or a service achieves its objectives. First half of the quality cycle. Related term is **quality assessment**.
Quality assurance	Process whereby consumers or clients can be guaranteed that products are fit for their purpose or that a service will achieve its objectives. The activities or procedures needed to make sure standards are achieved and thus that consumers or clients can be given such a guarantee.
Quality assurance group	A team of people sharing responsibility for the establishment and operation of quality assurance procedures.
Quality chain	Series of relationships between customers and suppliers involving quality considerations; can involve an individual being both supplier and customer.
Quality circle	Group of people sharing responsibility for quality initiatives; can involve people working in different organizational locations or in the same location.
Quality control	Systems for monitoring the quality of products through statistical analysis of levels of quality achieved; operates by inspecting samples of goods once they have been produced.

Quality management	Design, development, facilitation and support of quality systems, particularly in complex organizations (see 'total quality management' below).
Quality policy	Coherent statement of broad principles underpinning the development and operation of quality systems and procedures.
Quality system	Organization-wide set of procedures for overall assurance of quality; includes explicit allocations of responsibility and procedures for the flow of information between different parts of the system.
Stakeholder	Individual having a personal interest; in social care includes clients, professionals, managers and the various groups and bodies responsible for funding and resource decisions.
Standard	A statement specifying expected or desired attributes of a product or service. Usually taken to be less specific than a criterion.
Structure quality	The extent to which the physical and human resources available for care and the organizational settings in which they are deployed meet specified standards.
Subjective	Influenced by thoughts, attitudes or opinions of observers; individual; difficult for observers to agree upon.
Technical	Aspects of care involving physical intervention; care tasks requiring specialist professional knowledge but not involving face-to-face interaction with clients.
Threshold standards	Standards specifying minimum acceptable quality; standards below which quality must not fall.
Total quality management	Approach to quality management which emphasizes the involvement of all employees in quality activities; also suggests that the development of a quality 'culture' in which each employee is personally committed to quality improvement is more important than any specific quality system.

Useful reading

Audit Commission (1992) *The Community Revolution: personal social services and community care*. HMSO, London.

Carr-Hill R. and Dalley, G. (1991) *Quality management initiatives in the NHS*. Booklets 1 to 4. Centre for Health Economics, University of York, York.

Cassam, E. and Gupta, H. (1992) *Quality assurance for social care agencies*. Longman, London.

Cheetham, J., Fuller, R., McIvor, G. and Petch, A. (1992) *Evaluating social work effectiveness*. Open University Press, Buckingham.

Department of Health (1997) *The new NHS*. HMSO, London.

Department of Health Social Services Inspectorate (1991) *Inspecting for quality*. HMSO, London.

Di Primio, A. (1987) *Quality assurance in service organisations*. Chilton, Radnor.

Dixon, P. and Carr-Hill, R. (1989) *The NHS and its customers. Booklet Two. Customer feedback surveys – an introduction to survey methods*. Centre for Health Economics, University of York, York.

Donabedian, A. (1966) Evaluating the quality of medical care. *Milbank Memorial Fund Quarterly*, **44**, 166–206.

Donabedian, A. (1985) Twenty years of research on the quality of medical care. *Evaluation and the Health Professions* **8**, 243–265.

Donabedian, A. (1986) Quality assurance: corporate responsibility for multi-hospital systems. *Quality Review Bulletin*, **12**, 3–7.

Ellis, R. (ed) (1988) *Professional competence and quality assurance in the caring professions*. Croom Helm, Beckenham.

Ellis, R. and Whittington, D. (1993) *Quality assurance in health care: a handbook*. Edward Arnold, London.

Garvin, D.A. (1988) *Managing quality: the strategic and competitive edge*. Collier Macmillan, New York.

James, A. (1992) *Committed to quality*. HMSO and King's Fund, London.

Kelly, D. and Warr, B. (eds) (1992) *Quality counts: achieving quality in social care services*. Whiting and Birch, London.

Kemp, N. and Richardson, E. (1995) *Quality assurance in nursing practice* (2nd Edn.). Butterworth–Heinemann, London.

Kitson, A.L., Hyndman, S.J., Harvey, G. and Yerrell, P. (1990) *Quality patient care: an introduction to the RCN Dynamic Standard-Setting System (DySSSy)*. Scutari Press, London.

McIver, S. (1991–1996) *Obtaining the Views (1–6)*. King's Fund, London.

Oppenheim, A.N. (1986) *Questionnaire design and attitude measurement*. Gower, Aldershot.

Palmer, R.H., Donabedian, A. and Povar, G.J. (1991) *Striving for quality in health care*. Health Administration Press, Ann Arbor, MI.

Pfeffer, N. (1991) *Is Quality Good for You?: A critical review of quality in welfare*. Social Policy Paper Five. Institute for Public Policy Research, London.

Royal College of Nursing (1990) *The Dynamic Standards Setting System*. Royal College of Nursing, London.

Rust, R. and Oliver, R. (1994) *Service quality: new directions in theory and practice*. Sage Publications, Thousand Oaks, CA.

Stricker, F. and Rodriguez, A. (1988) *Handbook of quality assurance in mental health*. Plenum, New York.

Wilson, C.R.M. (1987) *Hospital-wide quality assurance: models for implementation and development*. W.B. Saunders, Toronto.

References

Argyle, M. (1969) *Social interaction*. Methuen, London.

Cassam, E. and Gupta, H. (1992) *Quality assurance for social care agencies*. Longman, London.

Department of Health (1989) *Homes are for living in: a model for evaluating quality of care provided*. HMSO, London.

Department of Health (1997) *The new NHS*. HMSO, London.

Donabedian, A. (1966) Evaluating the quality of medical care. *Milbank Memorial Fund Quarterly*, **44**, 166–206.

Donabedian, A. (1986) Quality assurance: corporate responsibility for multi-hospital systems. *Quality Review Bulletin*, **12**, 3–7.

Ellis, R. and Whittington, D. (1993) *Quality assurance in health care: a handbook*. Edward Arnold, London.

James, A. (1992) *Committed to quality*. HMSO and King's Fund, London.

Juran, J.M. (ed.) (1988) *Juran's quality control handbook*, 4th edn. McGraw-Hill, New York.

Knapp, M. (1984) *The economics of social care*. Macmillan, London.

Maxwell, R.J. (1984) Quality assessment in health. *British Medical Journal* **288**, 1470–1471.

Royal College of Nursing (1990) *The Dynamic Standards Setting System*. Royal College of Nursing, London.

Whittington, D., Gibson, F., Serplus, B., McCallion, G. and Kane, K. (1994) *An evaluation of intensive domiciliary care schemes in the Eastern Health and Social Services Board*. Centre for Health and Social Research, University of Ulster, Coleraine.

Wistow, G., Knapp, M., Hardy, B., Forder, J., Kendall, J. and Manning, R. (1996) *Social care markets: progress and prospects*. Open University Press, Buckingham.

Author Index

Subject Index